(New) Fascism

Breakthroughs in Mimetic Theory

Edited by William A. Johnsen

(New) Fascism
Contagion, Community, Myth

Nidesh Lawtoo

Michigan State University Press

East Lansing

♾ The paper used in this publication meets the minimum requirements
of ANSI/NISO Z39.48-1992 (R 1997) (Permanence of Paper).

Michigan State University Press
East Lansing, Michigan 48823-5245

This project has received funding from the European Research Council (ERC) under the
European Union's Horizon 2020 research and innovation program (grant agreement No.
716181: HOM). The author is solely responsible for the views expressed in this book.

Printed and bound in the United States of America.

28 27 26 25 24 23 22 21 20 19   1 2 3 4 5 6 7 8 9 10

Library of Congress Cataloging-in-Publication Data
Names: Lawtoo, Nidesh, author.
Title: (New) fascism : contagion, community, myth / Nidesh Lawtoo.
Description: East Lansing, Mich. : Michigan State University Press, 2019.
| Includes bibliographical references.
Identifiers: LCCN 2018050616| ISBN 9781611863291 (pbk. : alk. paper)
| ISBN 9781609176082 (pdf) | ISBN 9781628953718 (epub) | ISBN 9781628963724 (kindle)
Subjects: LCSH: Fascism — Philosophy.
Classification: LCC JC481 .L39 2019 | DDC 320.53/3 — dc23
LC record available at https://lccn.loc.gov/2018050616

Cover and book design by Erin Kirk New
Composition by Charlie Sharp, Sharp Des!gns, East Lansing, Michigan
Cover art © Ali Mazraie Shadi. All rights reserved.

Michigan State University Press is a member of the Green Press Initiative and is
committed to developing and encouraging ecologically responsible publishing
practices. For more information about the Green Press Initiative and the use of
recycled paper in book publishing, please visit www.greenpressinitiative.org.

Visit Michigan State University Press at www.msupress.org

Ur-Fascism can come back under the most innocent of disguises. Our duty is to uncover it and to point our finger at any of its new instances—every day, in every part of the world.

Umberto Eco, "Ur-Fascism"

Contents

Foreword

Mikkel Borch-Jacobsen

Readers beware: this is not your usual academic book. It is a very forceful, thought-provoking, and timely intervention in a political context dominated by the rise of new forms of fascism, notably in the United States, but also elsewhere in the world.

Nidesh Lawtoo does not shy away from the term "fascism," but he doesn't use it lightly. Rather, he shows how our usual "enlightened" political categories and reflexes prevent us from recognizing fascism in the first place. For this political philosophy rooted in the subject of *Aufklärung*, Lawtoo substitutes another, much less optimistic theoretical tradition, that of mimesis.

For this longstanding tradition that goes all the way back to Plato's *Republic*, what we Moderns call the "subject" or the "ego" is originally a copy, a shadow of other people. Far from being autonomous and "rational animals," we are essentially social beings whose thoughts, but also behavior, character, affects, and desires are shaped mimetically—an age-old intuition that finds support, Lawtoo claims, in the recent discovery of "mirror neurons" that trigger the reflex imitation of other people's gestures and expressions. The immediate implication of all this, as Plato well understood, is that we are fundamentally malleable, suggestible, and that this mimetic modeling is "beyond good and evil": it can be used to shape rational and ethical citizens, but it can also degenerate into irrational psychic contagion and mass hysteria—that is, into what late nineteenth-century theorists called "crowd psychology."

Lawtoo expertly retraces the theories of the major proponents of the mimetic theory from Plato to Girard through Nietzsche, Tarde, Le Bon, Freud, Bataille, Lacoue-Labarthe, and Nancy, and he shows how, taken together, they allow us to diagnose and understand the current fascist "pathology" much better than the usual liberal or progressive discourse. Lawtoo's will not be the first book to cry "fascism" à propos

Trump (Madeleine Albright and Timothy Snyder come to mind), but it is the first to provide a theory that is equal to the task of explaining how and why a neo-fascist clown managed to get elected president of a democracy such as the United States of America.

Lawtoo's account is both incredibly enlightening and incredibly sobering as it forces us to face the mimetic beast in all of us, the old and new "Man of the Crowds." The passages in which Lawtoo illustrates the mimetic theory with the current political situation in the United States are always right on target, and I only wish there were more of them, as they are so telling and provide the public with a key to what is happening here and now.

Readers beware: Ye who enter, abandon all illusions. . . .

among us children on the courtyard of our school, but when it was used—as a fight would escalate, for instance, or as a bully would boss us around—it inevitably triggered an automatic reflex in the accused to set up a maximum distance from whatever reality this obscure accusation may have designated in the past—in a country that, despite the proximity, we felt, was not *our* country anyway.

Childhood impressions can be lasting. Three decades later, completing a PhD in another country far from home, I still had no particular desire to study a political phenomenon that didn't seem likely to return in any democratic country any time soon, and that concerned something that had happened long ago, far away—over that border. If the word itself still conveyed the pathos we had sensed in childhood, now intensified by a deeper knowledge of the horrors that had actually taken place, the political reality felt more distant than ever, both in time and space. True, George W. Bush had just won the 2000 presidential election against Al Gore, in a hotly contested nomination, but I was in the United States of America after all, "the land of the free," and if the political, economic, and cultural climate was far from stable, there appeared to be no immediate danger looming on the horizon.

But was this appearance real? As I progressively familiarized myself with the affective and infective register fascist leaders had once employed to galvanize crowds in the past, relying on rhetorical techniques that included authoritarian affirmation, repetition of nationalist slogans, use of images rather than thoughts, clear-cut division between good and evil, chosen and not chosen people, us and them, among other disquieting hierarchical distinctions, I felt somewhat uneasy and began to wonder: could these old phantoms return, perhaps under new masks?

Meanwhile, the topic of behavioral imitation (or *mimesis*), which had mediated the affective relation between fascist leaders and the suggestible crowds in the 1920s and 1930s, was becoming interesting for scholarly reasons as well. It seemed to render manifest symptoms that were otherwise latent in the modernist literary and philosophical texts I was reading, but immediately emerged as I placed the texts within a broader historical and theoretical context—irrational symptoms like affective contagion and automatic reflexes, hypnotic spells and hysterical dispossessions, violent actions and mirroring, unconscious reactions.

I thus began to wonder about the relation between the unconscious and crowd behavior, which seemed to play such a key role in the emergence of fascist movements. In my home fields, literary theory and philosophy, psychoanalysis still provided the dominant frame to solve what Sigmund Freud, a few years before the rise of fascism, had famously called "the riddle" of group formation, and I explored that well-traveled route. At the same time, a minor pre-Freudian tradition among modernist "philosophical physicians" I was progressively uncovering urged me to ask a different question: namely, could it be that embodied forms of automatic imitation, or mimicry, perhaps more than dreams, provided, if not a *via regia*, at least a backdoor to an unconscious that was not only personal but also collective, not solely psychological but also physio-psychological, not based on a repressive hypothesis but on a mimetic hypothesis?

I did not have any clear answers at the time, but a change of perspective was already underway. Hence, what had started as an inquiry into the psychic life of the ego progressively morphed into a diagnostic of mimetic crowds that had the power to turn the ego into a copy, shadow, or, to echo Nietzsche's diagnostic phrase, a "phantom of the ego."[1]

This move, I later realized, was not original. It was in line with a long-standing tradition in Western thought that goes all the way back to the origins of mimetic theory, in Plato's *Republic*. This tradition stresses that mimesis and the "phantoms" (*phantasmata*) it generates are as much visual as they are affective, insofar as these phantoms do not remain confined within the walls of representation at the bottom of a mythic cave. Rather, as Plato was the first to fear, they also cast a spell on viewers, shaping the *ethos* of a subject, of a people, and, eventually, of a city or a state. Plato, of course, advocates for the imitation of good, rational, and ideal models, but he was also the first to realize that mimesis cuts both ways, urging future philosophical physicians not to forget the irrational power of affective contamination. Whether he would have appreciated the irony that the *Republic* was one of the texts Mussolini kept on his desk during the last days of fascism, I cannot say—for an undeniable anti-democratic bent in his thought is balanced by an equally undeniable the paradigmatic case study that framed the whole project, insofar as he considers Wagner a "case" that is not only personal and psychological but also collective and political. Why? Because his former model occupies the place of what Nietzsche calls, contra Wagner, a "leader" (*Führer*) who has the power to "hypnotize" the "masses" (*Massen*).

But strikingly similar evaluations appeared on the side of literature, or, to use a more ancient term, myth as well: in Joseph Conrad's account of Kurtz in *Heart of Darkness* (1899) as a "leader" who, while "hollow at the core," "electrified large meetings" "on the popular side," for instance; or in D. H. Lawrence's dramatization of European aristocratic leaders in *The Plumed Serpent* (1926) who reenacted mythic and sacrificial rituals that cast a "spell" on the "crowd" in New Mexico; or, closer to Western horrors, in Georges Bataille's attention to the "Psychological Structure of Fascism" (1933/34) centered on "leaders" (*meneurs*) that generate hypnotic movements of "attraction and repulsion" in modern societies, monocephalic societies that, he controversially argued, should be rendered *acéphale*—that is, deprived of a head or leader.[2]

Such modernist accounts, I argued in the company of key contemporary figures in mimetic theory such as René Girard, Philippe Lacoue-Labarthe, and Mikkel Borch-Jacobsen, foresaw the rise of fascism and Nazism in the 1920s and 1930s, and called attention to the dangerous role played by mimetic affects in triggering fascist and Nazi politics in the past century. I had thus been hooked on mimetic theory for scholarly reasons that explained a disconcerting political phenomenon, a contagious phenomenon that did not fit within dominant accounts of the subject of *Aufklärung* (the Enlightenment).

And yet—and here comes the confession—in the wake of 9/11, of the political lies, the crusades, the media simulations, and the real invasions that ensued, I could not help but notice the power, if not of fascist governments or regimes as such, at least of the *mimetic pathos* traditionally mobilized by fascist leaders who relied on authoritarian affirmation, aggressive nationalism, scapegoating mechanisms, and spectacular lies among other rhetorical techniques to cast a hypnotic spell on the crowd. This spell, amplified by the aptly named "mass media," did not put our critical faculties entirely to sleep, and a significant segment of the population resisted it. And yet, while still far removed, the phantom of fascism seemed to cast a looming shadow on one of the major democracies in the West at the dawn of the present century—a suspicion aggravated by the increasing popularity of far-right, neo-fascist movements in Europe as well.

I was often traveling back and forth over the Atlantic, and I could see that this was a shared concern. Having spent two years doing research in France, I could hear from friends they were still shocked that the far-right leader of the National Front, Jean-Marie Le Pen, a Holocaust denier, had come in second in the first round of France's 2002 presidential elections. The revival of nationalist movements on the far right was also taking place in Germany, the Netherlands, Austria, and England, among other countries whose democracies were put to the test by the increasing number of refugees in need of asylum supplemented by growing austerity measures.

Closer to home, Italy, under the spell of Silvio Berlusconi—whose slogan, *Forza Italia!*, capitalized on a national sport to generate enthusiasm in the crowd—was already "ahead" of the game. If only because it provided a striking example of the power of mass media to turn politics itself into a game. The game had, of course, real effects. Italy's economic crisis, its generalized institutional corruption, and the so-called brain drain that ensued were but some of the symptoms my Italian friends complained about. It was also a confirmation of Umberto Eco's warning that "behind a regime and its ideology there is always a way of thinking and feeling, a group of cultural habits, of obscure instincts and unfathomable drives." These mimetic drives had led Eco to ask what appeared as an untimely question in 1995: "Is there still another ghost stalking Europe (not to speak of other parts of the world)?"[3] What I know is that even my former school friends in Switzerland, who, by then, had their own children on the school's courtyard, no longer felt completely immune in my home "neutral" country either—despite the border.

This brief autobiographical sketch helps perhaps to partially explain why the realization that a phantom haunts the contemporary political scene already in-*formed* (gave form to) the readings of philosophical and literary texts that animated what then became *The Phantom of the Ego* (2013).

It left diagnostics behind of what I called fascist "patho(-) logies," understood both as a form of pathological affective contagion (or pathology) and as a critical *logos* on mimetic *pathos* (or patho-logy) central to the psychology of fascism, a mimetic psychology that, I was convinced by then, haunted the contemporary political scene as well.

And yet, by the time the book appeared, this double-faced diagnostic seemed somewhat out of joint with the general political climate of the times, for the electoral pendulum had finally swung, at least in the United States. And as the first African American president gifted with a double cultural identity was elected, and then reelected, everything seemed possible again: for, "yes," we enthusiastically chanted—"we can!" . . . Or at least we could, until another phantom took office and decided to "make America great again."

Many of us have been wondering since: how could a liberating dream turn into a political nightmare? Mimetic theory, I should say at the outset, does not have the only key to solve this riddle. Still, it provides a specific diagnostic of the affective, hypnotic, and contagious power (or *pathos*) fascist leaders have used in the past to cast a spell on the masses, a mimetic spell which, we are beginning to realize, can always be reloaded in the present and future, my country or your country.

From these prefatory remarks, it should be clear that my approach to fascism will be necessarily partial and selective; it takes the increasingly influential, yet still little understood phenomenon of imitation (or mimesis) as an Ariadne's thread to orient ourselves in the labyrinth of (new) fascist movements. As the subtitle specifies, it traces the genealogy of three related mimetic concepts that were once central to the spread of fascist pathos—contagion, community, and myth—and are now proving central to the rise of new fascism as well.

While different doors could have been selected to access the affective and infective sources of fascist will to power, these three had a double advantage: on one side, they allowed me to inscribe this diagnostic in a chain of influential thinkers of mimesis—from Plato to Nietzsche, Bataille to Girard—who are attentive to the irrational, violent, and unconscious power of imitative behavior that is currently at play on the political scene; on the other, related, side these concepts open up new interdisciplinary connections for mimetic theory by drawing on recent developments in disciplines as diverse as continental philosophy, psychology, anthropology, history, political theory, as well as the neurosciences—all disciplines that testify to the urgency to rethink the ancient problem of mimesis in light of current political crises.

If this little book contributes to bringing back to the theoretical scene a protean and quite influential concept that has been marginalized in theoretical debates still informed by the linguistic turn in the 1970s and 1980s, was once considered central to the rise of fascist leaders in the 1920s and 1930s, and is all too visibly center stage today, it will have accomplished its goal.

The essays that compose the book were written under time pressure in order to confront the threat of rising candidates on the far right in presidential elections that were still ongoing, both in Europe and the United States, when I started writing. I first presented chapter 2 at a conference on community at the University of Bern at the beginning of November 2016, a week before the results of the U.S.

presidential election were announced. I would not say that I predicted the results, but I regret I did not have to modify the argument. Chapter 3 was presented at a French conference at Trinity College, Dublin, in May 2017, a few weeks before Marine Le Pen—who, like her father, came in second in the first round—failed to be elected as France's president. We were relieved, but we also sensed that the power of nationalist, racist, and fascist myths continues to cast a shadow on Europe, the West, and beyond. The conversation with political theorist William Connolly in the Coda took place in Weimar, Germany, one month later, not far from a now peaceful square where Hitler assembled massive crowds. Chapter 1 on crowd behavior was added in the fall of 2017 when I belatedly realized that this geographical trajectory could be assembled in a little book that would supplement a mimetic perspective to the growing number of dissenting voices. Whether it can serve as an antidote contra the (re)election of pathological phantoms that are destined to vanish soon, yet will always threaten to return under different masks, only the future will tell.

Acknowledgments

This book could not have been written without the long tradition of mimetic theorists on which it stands and the generous support of the European Research Council, which is currently funding the *Homo Mimeticus* (HOM) project, of which *(New) Fascism* is part. Given the genealogical method I inherit, I happily show my gratitude by acknowledging my debts to this mimetic tradition, quoting from its main advocates, while furthering their lines of thought. The reader will find their names—too numerous to mention here—in the pages that follow.

There are other names I would like to mention at the outset, for they are part of a vibrant intellectual community I feel privileged to belong to. I warmly thank Mikkel Borch-Jacobsen, Bill Connolly, Jane Bennett, and Adriana Cavarero for numerous transatlantic conversations that left traces in this book; Ortwin de Graef, Roland Breeur, Julia Jansen, Tom Toremans, Sascha Bru, the MDRN team, my HOM team members, Niki Hadikoesoemo and Daniel Villegas Vélez, and all the participants of the *Homo Mimeticus* Seminar for joining forces to forge new interdisciplinary/mimetic connections at KU Leuven, Belgium; Hannes Opelz, for inviting me to Trinity College to speak about the "power of myth" *à partir de* Lacoue-Labarthe; and Jean-Luc Nancy for sharing his thoughts with the HOM team in a memorable workshop on *Le mythe nazi*—in a communal sprit of *partage*.

Last but not least, my deepest gratitude goes to my editor at MSU Press, Bill Johnsen, for welcoming this book in the Breakthroughs in Mimetic Theory series, and to my partner, Michi Lawtoo, for giving me the original idea to write it in the first place—provided, she added, that I "keep it short."

At least I tried.

Introduction

> It is thus that the maddest and most interesting
> ages of history always emerge, when the "actors," *all*
> kinds of actors, become the real masters.
> —Friedrich Nietzsche, *The Gay Science*

What times allow actors to play the role that previously belonged to masters? And wherein lies these actors' power to turn what would normally be considered madness into interesting, but also dangerous ages? These questions are not new. Since classical antiquity actors have been defined as protean figures endowed with a power to cast a spell on all kinds of theaters, including political theaters, thereby blurring the line between appearance and reality, fiction and truth, playing a role and being that role. And yet, it is only relatively recently that Nietzsche's prophetic diagnostic has become quite literally true, and "*all* kinds of actors"[1] have turned into political masters that haunt, phantom-like, the contemporary world. Hence the renewed urgency of his untimely call for new unmasking operations to grasp the power of mimetic pathos.

This actor qua master cannot be framed within a stable, rational identity that tells us, once and for all, what its essential character is, should be, or is likely to become. And yet, precisely for this reason, this figure with an identity that is not singular but plural has attracted the interest of protean thinkers who have themselves mastered a few mimetic tricks. My hypothesis in what follows is that a Nietzschean strand in mimetic theory that is affectively implicated in the forms of theatrical mastery it denounces can paradoxically help us, if not to univocally define, at least to begin unmasking contemporary actors who impersonate fictional roles of authority on all kinds of political stages, casting a real shadow on the contemporary world.

The Shadow of Fascism

History does not repeat itself, but sometimes it is said to rhyme; and when it rhymes, the echoes can potentially generate re-productions of horrors we thought we had long left behind. Perhaps not fascism "itself," then, but the *shadow* of fascism has recently manifested itself on the contemporary political scene.

Arguably, its most spectacular manifestation appeared in the United States as Donald J. Trump, an entertainer of a reality television show acting as a billionaire businessman, won, against all expectations, the 2016 presidential election and turned his TV show into a political reality. His victory, it must be emphasized, came *without* the support of the popular vote and does not accurately reflect the political views of the majority of the U.S. population—far from it.

Still, it signaled a certain failure of democratic institutions that favor the election of figures who can self-fund their campaigns. It also illustrated the success of an aggressively nationalist, racist, and violent rhetoric that, if dramatically enacted by an actor trained in the sphere of fiction, could easily turn the political itself into a fiction. Donald Trump, in fact, effectively exploited the political stage, amplified by the mass media to generate mass enthusiasm in physical crowds and virtual publics. Paradoxically, this show was particularly effective in casting a spell on the white working-class section of the population. That is, a disenfranchised, suffering population that could be tricked into a mimetic relation with the very fictional model of oppression responsible for their real disenfranchisement.

The paradoxical logic of mimetic pathos (or patho-logy), as we shall see, does not rest on a rational discourse (or *logos*) that conforms to the norms of waking consciousness. Rather, it triggers mirroring affects with far-reaching, infective (or pathological) effects that are channeled via what I call the mimetic unconscious. This unconscious is mimetic in the sense that it leads people—most visibly when assembled in a crowd or a public, but not only—to involuntarily mimic, feel, and reproduce the affects of the leader qua model. This also means that the mimetic unconscious does not require interpretations of personal dreams to become manifest. Instead, it calls for careful diagnostics of real, intersubjective relations central to social and political behavior; mimicry, emotional contagion, hypnosis, vulnerability to suggestion, lowering of rational faculties, subordination of thought to drives (especially sexual and violent drives), and a general inability to discern between truth and lies are some of its most visible manifestations.[2]

While these mimetic symptoms are most visibly at play on the North American political scene, I hasten to add that this mimetic danger cannot be confined to the United States alone. Quite the contrary. Consider the rise of far-right movements in Europe that reload fascist ideals of national purity, most visibly in France (The National Front), the Netherlands (Party for Freedom), Germany (Alternative for Deutschland), Italy (The League), to name a few; the far-right anti-immigration policies in the UK (Brexit); not to speak of non-Western oligarchies (most visibly North Korea and Russia) that are caught in relations of both mirroring complicity and escalating reciprocity with the current U.S. administration, and, as historian Timothy Snyder has recently shown, are currently paving the way for "the road to unfreedom."[3]

This road away from freedom that the West is currently taking is a powerful reminder that, in a globalized, mediatized, and hyperconnected world, new forms of (fascist) political pathologies do not stop at national borders—let alone walls. Instead, in the age of the Internet, they spread contagiously, via a proliferation of new, transnational media and the cyberwars they trigger. These hypermimetic wars dissolve not only the very conception of clearly defined borders, but also the ontological distinction between self and others, originals and copies, truths and lies, virtual attacks and real attacks.

Still, the recent case of Trump in the United States provides an interesting case study to diagnose the political power of mimesis as it circulates from the masses to the leader and back, generating collective movements that will outlive their leaders and need to be studied, for at least two reasons. First, because this case reveals that even a country that served as a bastion of democracy contra the external threat of fascism in the past century can potentially capitulate to uncannily similar temptations in the present century. Rather than projecting the threat of fascism outside, beyond national borders, we are thus encouraged to reflect on its threat from the inside—for *no country is immune from fascist contagion*. A blind belief in immunity can actually prevent the population from seeing that an infection has already taken place.

And second, the case of the United States qualifies as "interesting" in the Nietzschean sense because, not for the first time, a democratic process has turned an actor trained to captivate an audience in a fictional world into a political leader with power over the real world. Unsurprisingly, what I call the "apprentice president," to evoke the popular reality-television show Trump hosted (*The Apprentice*) before being elected, turned out to be quite trained in playing the role of a fictional president. In particular, he used the same mimetic skills—amplified by new media that, in the digital age, make the power of fascism more insidious, ramified, and pervasive—to cast a hypnotic spell on voters in the real world, blurring the boundaries between the private and the public, but also reality and fiction, truth and lies, conscious actions and unconscious reactions.

Rather than dismissing the mimetic power of actors as fictional, we are thus encouraged to consider that fictions do not remain within the boundary of realistic representations. Rather, they affect and infect—via forms of mimetic contagion that operate on the unconscious register of passions, or pathos—the psychic lives of spectators who are both attracted and repelled by mimetic pathologies in need of new diagnostic operations.

Fascism, Old and New

For these and other reasons, we are confronted with an exemplary case study to diagnose the mimetic techniques of "populist" leaders that a growing number of dissident voices in political theory have started to designate as "neofascist," "aspirational fascist," or "new fascist" leaders.[4]

If we have become accustomed to relegating fascist politics to an unfortunate chapter of European history, or if the term fascist may seem overtly alarmist to talk about what could be considered a simple manifestation of "populism," Umberto Eco's penetrating account of the key characteristics of what he calls "Ur-Fascism" or "Eternal Fascism" should give us pause for thought. As Eco puts it, recurring features of that protean phenomenon that is fascism include, among other symptoms, "a cult of tradition," "irrationalism," "fear of difference," "appeal to a frustrated middle class," "action for action's sake," "machismo," and a type of "impoverished vocabulary," or Newspeak, that, he warns us as early as 1995, can be mediated by a new type of "Internet populism" that has the power to turn the voice of the people into a "theatrical fiction."[5] Prescient in theoretical insights very few could foresee at the twilight of the twentieth century, the effectiveness of Internet fictions is now put into political practice for all to see at the dawn of the twenty-first century.

More recently, new dissenting voices have given historical and theoretical confirmations of Eco's premonition that the phantom of fascism may return to haunt the twenty-first century. Timothy Snyder's historical reminder in *On Tyranny* (2017) is worth bearing in mind. As he puts it, "There is little reason to think that we are ethically superior to the European of the 1930s and 1940s, or for that matter less vulnerable to the kind of ideas that Hitler successfully promulgated and realized."[6] This is an uncomfortable truth that is essential leaders with authoritarian inclinations than to the media used to disseminate them. Either way, on both sides of the medium/message divide, mimesis continues to play a key role on the political scene.

Since what I call, for lack of a more original term, "(new) fascism" rests on mimetic mechanisms I first uncovered by diagnosing the affective will to power of "old" fascist leaders in the 1920s and '30s, genealogical lenses will make us see that the distinction between "old" and "new" fascism will not be stable and watertight, and for at least two reasons. First, as historians have repeatedly pointed out, fascism is far from being the unitary phenomenon the singular term suggests, assumes different forms in different countries, and escapes essentialist definitions of what fascism was, is, or aims to become. And second, because what I group under the rubric of "(new) fascism" is a heterogeneous, transnational phenomenon that is currently emerging as I write, manifests itself differently in different countries plagued by specific national problems (economic crises, income inequality, immigration crises, racism, etc.), and generates unpredictable twists and turns on a daily basis with the intention of triggering chaos while progressively undermining democratic principles.

For these two related reasons, I refrain from fictionally adopting an omniscient perspective that would set up a clear-cut opposition between "old" and "new" fascism under the false assumption that they would designate stable, unitary, and clearly differentiated phenomena one could isolate and compare from a safe theoretical distance.

And yet, this does not mean that a comparative approach between old and new forms of fascist pathos is out of place. Precisely because of its indeterminacy, I consider it essential to step back to the fascism of the 1920s, '30s, and '40s to come to grips with new fascist pathologies that are currently emerging. We can in fact learn a good deal from the specific methods fascist leaders used to inject irrational affects (*pathoi*) in crowds in the past, and from the mimetic discourses (*logoi*) these leaders rely on, in order to diagnose both old and new fascist pathologies that are spreading contagiously in the present.[10]

For this second, comparative operation a more fluid, perspectival, genealogical, or as I also call it, patho-*logical* method is in order. If patho-logy looks back to fascist theories and practices of the past, its goal is not to find stable origins, laws, or definitions that would frame a protean phenomenon whose primary characteristic is that it defies singular identifications. Rather, its goal is to uncover genealogical continuities and discontinuities relevant to account for specific forms of mimetic communication that are currently playing a leading role in the reemergence of new fascist phantoms that cast a shadow on the present and future.

I adopt a genealogical method for a series of reasons that will become progressively clear, but one should be mentioned at the outset. Never has Nietzsche's opening line of *The Genealogy of Morals* rung truer than today: "We remain unknown to ourselves" (*Wir sind uns unbekannt*).[11] For Nietzsche, this state of non-knowledge, which includes the "seekers of knowledge," becomes particularly visible when "everyone is furthest from himself," a psychic state of dispossession he often designated as the "herd-instinct."[12] This mimetic, all too mimetic instinct makes subjects who are assembled in a crowd (but not only those) vulnerable to tyrannical figures who, Nietzsche continues, have the power that has been known since Plato and Aristotle that defines *Homo sapiens* as the most imitative species. Humans are, in fact, thoroughly mimetic, not only in the sense that we create aesthetic representations of reality (though we do that too), but in the more fundamental psychological, sociological, and political sense that we mimic the behavior of others—a tendency that, since the discovery of mirror neurons in the 1990s, first in monkeys and then in humans as well, has been receiving growing confirmations from the neurosciences and is currently contributing to a better understanding of a thoroughly mimetic species I call *Homo mimeticus*.

Mimetic theory balances positivist accounts of the subject that stress the role imitation plays in understanding others as it teaches us that mimesis cuts both ways and can be put to rational and irrational uses. Fascist leaders certainly exploited the mimetic irrationality of crowds to come to power. In this context, the mimetic language of contagion, spells, and hypnotic influences to account for crowd behavior remains particularly important. It should not be too quickly dismissed as a remnant of the "old" fascism, for it continues to be at play in new fascism as well. As Timothy into what I call hypermimesis. To identify the newness of (new) fascism, a change of perspective is in order. What is new, in fact, might not primarily reside in the ideological content of leaders' programs, which is far from being original. As they aspire to occupy authoritarian positions of power, they echo well-known hypernationalist, racist, homophobic, authoritarian, and aggressively militarist messages that are, in themselves, not new—though these chilling messages remain the most visible symptoms that allow us to identify the reappearance of fascist tendencies on the political scene we should not simply dismiss as populist. Construction of walls, promotion of racism, homophobia, mimicry of fascist dictators, collusion with fascist oligarchs, dissemination of fear, increase of inequalities, dismantling of public services, religious bans, threats of nuclear escalation, institution of camps, imprisonment of children, etc.—these are all fascist symptoms that are not new; they certainly work against the population, undermine basic human rights, and cast a dark shadow on freedom and democracy more generally.

What is new in fascism might be less on the side of the *message* and more on the side of leaders' use of the *media*, including new social media that not only disseminate political fictions but turn politics itself into a fiction. To be sure, (new) fascist leaders continue to rely on the same rhetorical techniques to arouse crowds and spread their messages. But more importantly, in the digital age, in addition to traditional sources of news, like newspapers, radio, and television, leaders with authoritarian tendencies can now rely on new Internet-based social media like Facebook and Twitter, which expose the population to an incessant flow of simulated information that does not even attempt to represent reality, lets go of referential facts, and operates as a mode of entertainment characteristic of hypermimetic fictions.

Hypermimesis, then, continues to rest on the psychic laws of imitations, but pushes them to extremes, blurring ontological distinctions between fiction and reality, copy and origins, truth and lies. And yet, this does not mean that these digital fictions are deprived of effects on real life, which are at least double: on the one hand, in the hands of authoritarian leaders, new media threaten to dissolve the ontological distinction between truth and lies, appearance and reality, on which the traditional laws of mimesis rest, generating hyperreal shadows without any referent that absorb the real in the alternative sphere of the virtual; on the other, related hand, these shadows retroact on spectators and users who, under the spell of an incessant politics of entertainment that reinforces already held beliefs, suspend disbelief and subordinate the difficult search for truth[1] (or *logos*) to the facile enjoyment of affect (or *pathos*) generating hypermimetic pathologies that spread contagiously from the virtual to the real world and back—in an endless spiral that turns shadows into realities, and the ego into a shadow or phantom of the ego.

This process of hypermimetic dispossession plays a double role in the rise of (new) fascist leaders. Once fictional phantoms have taken possession of the ego, on the one hand, and shadows are mistaken for reality, on the other, subjects are no longer driven by rational consciousness but by the mimetic unconscious instead. This also means that a hypermimetic subject who is exposed to daily "breaking news" (true or fake) via mass media (old and new) that are specifically designed (by humans or algorithms) to reinforce and radicalize an already entrenched ideological position, *is not primarily concerned with the question of truth* (logos)*, but with the generation of affect* (pathos) *instead*. What ensues are collective pathologies that catch the new media consumer in a widening spiral of virtual simulations that are not simply hyperreal and disconnected from reality; on the contrary, they have the hypermimetic power to bring (new) fascist phantoms into real life. Hence the need to step back to mimetic principles central to the rise of fascism in the past, in order to subsequently shed light on the hypermimetic principles at play in (new) fascism in the present and future.

In sum, my primary goal is not to give an account of contemporary (new) fascist leaders and the movements they generate on the basis of their politics, ideology, or *Weltanschauung* alone—for fascist ideology is notoriously variable, adaptable, and positions that might not initially appear to traditionally belong to fascism—such as climate-change denial for instance—could, with the benefit of hindsight, turn out to be responsible for the most horrific global consequences of (new) fascism. Nor is it to freeze a protean and moving phenomenon without a proper identity in a "the solidarity of committed militants."[19] After Mussolini founded the so-called Fasci di Combattimento in Milan in 1919, he adopted the symbol of the *fasces*, the Roman axe bound in rods, to signal a recuperation of a Roman imperial legacy endowed with sovereign power of life and death over its subjects.

The term was thus not original, but was based on the imitation of the ancients. As Mussolini put it in *La dottrina del fascismo* (written with the fascist philosopher Giovanni Gentile in 1932): "No doctrine can claim an absolute originality [*originalità assoluta*]. It is bound, if only historically, to the doctrines that once were and to the doctrines that will be."[20] There is thus a mimetic element internal to fascism that inevitably establishes a movement of repetition and difference between old and new elements of the *fascio*. While I agree with Kevin Passmore's historical claim that we can turn to fascism to "understand the past,"[21] I would also add that the main focus of a genealogical perspective is to return to the fascisms of the past in order to understand the emergence of new fascisms in the present.

Historically, it is worth remembering that the term

"fascism" had already been used by Sicilian peasants in the 1890s who had imbued the term with a "popular radicalism."[22] The term, and what it stood for, thus appealed to opposed constituencies; it was on the side of both the working people and a liberal elite, revolutionary and monarchic, conservative and progressive, nationalist and transnational, antimodern and premodern. In short, fascism can mean one thing and its very opposite, making a unitary, stable, and definitive definition of what fascism really means a contradiction in terms. Hence the importance of considering fascism as a process of becoming in constant transformation rather than as a fixed ideological essence.

Genealogically, it is equally worth stressing that the term "fascism" is, in itself, not without ambivalences, generating a contradictory dynamic that reaches into the present. Italian speakers would already have recognized that the axe of fascism cuts both ways, for it has both a positive and a negative side: namely, that *fascio* indicates unity since it serves as a *simbolo d'unità*, as Gentile put it; at the same time, it also implies the dissolution of individual differences into a unified bundle, or mass—a mimetic dissolution visually rendered in the Italian dictum *fare di tutta l'erba un fascio*, literally, to turn all the grass into a bundle. The implication being that if you're assembled in a *fascio*, it is no longer possible to identify the individual blades of grass, but also to discern the grass from the weed. In our language, in a *fascio* the ego has turned into a shadow or phantom of other egos.

Political unity and strength comes at the price of individual differentiation and freedom. As Mussolini continues in *La dottrina del fascismo* (1932), speaking of the twentieth century in terms that are not deprived of prophetic insights and should serve as a warning for the twenty-first century: "One can think that this is the century of authority, a century 'on the right,' a fascist century [*il secolo dell'autorità, un secolo di 'destra,' un secolo fascista*]."[23] And he adds: "If the 19th century was the century of the individual [*secolo dell'individuo*] . . . we are free to believe that this is the 'collective' century' [*secolo 'collettivo'*]."[24] Replacement of individual difference by collective sameness: this is, in a nutshell, the driving *telos* of fascism.

Interestingly, the transformation of differences into sameness is also one of the defining characteristics of mimesis. That is, a behavioral mimesis endowed with the power to fuse individual egos in a unitary movement, contagious community, or enthusiastic crowd generating an organic, undifferentiated, violent, and potentially warlike collective that comes awfully close to what René Girard calls a "mimetic crisis" or "loss of differences." Could it be, then, that the twenty-first century could potentially become a fascist century because it is already a mimetic or, better, hypermimetic century? This is a genealogical hypothesis we will explore in what follows.

Mimesis, then, understood both as imitation of past models and as imitation of other people that model themselves on authoritarian leaders, seems inscribed in the very semantic register of fascism. And yet, this does not mean that the mimetic principles fascist leaders trigger can be reduced to what Giovanni Gentile calls a "realistic doctrine" (*dottrina realistica*), which can easily be identified from a distance.

To delimit the territory and specify the diagnostic, what follows zeroes in on three distinct but related mimetic manifestations of pathos that cannot be dissociated from last decades of the nineteenth century specifically to study the mimetic and contagious behavior of crowds, and is linked to founding texts like Gustave Le Bon's *The Age of the Crowd* (1895) and Gabriel Tarde's *The Laws of Imitation* (1890), among others. Mimetic theory is a field of inquiry that emerged in the 1960s and is commonly associated with the work of René Girard; but its genealogy is much more ancient, goes all the way back to Plato and Aristotle, traverses the history of Western thought, and increasingly includes a heterogeneous number of figures and disciplines (philosophy, literary theory, anthropology, political theory, the neurosciences, among others) that are attentive to mimetic, and thus contagious, forms of human behavior that, in their real and virtual manifestations, are currently returning to the forefront of the theoretical and political scene.

Given the shared concerns between these two approaches, the few references to crowd psychology in mimetic theory are just as surprising as the lack of references to Girard in crowd psychology. In fact, both disciplines share a common concern with what is arguably the defining characteristic of *both* mimesis *and* fascism: that is, its contagious, affective dimension that blurs the boundary dividing not only truth from lies (the domain of philosophers), but also self from others (the domain of all humans).

Considering the recent success of leaders who effectively relied on mimetic contagion and hypnotic spells to come to power, there are thus ample reasons for strengthening the connection between these two exemplary disciplinary perspectives. This is especially true since, as I have noted, mimetic communication now operates not only via the medium of the mimetic crowd, or via print media, but also via new social media that radically amplify the hypnotic power of such leaders who can penetrate the way we think and feel via virtual, algorithmically based, yet not less contaminating technologies that have performative hypermimetic effects on real life.

The connection between crowd psychology and mimetic theory emerges naturally from the overlaps already internal to these traditions. If crowd psychology relies on the psychological notion of hypnotic "suggestion" to account for what Le Bon called the "contagious" dimension of affects to spread mimetically among a political crowd, Girard will implicitly recuperate this tradition by stressing the role of "mimesis" in the "contagious" propagation of violence in a ritual "community." The terms and contexts are different, yet they can easily be bridged if we realize that politics continues to rely on rituals, just as much as hypnosis continues to generate mirroring effects.

At the individual level, the link between mimesis and hypnosis has been noticed before. In a conversation with Girard, Jean-Michel Oughourlian considered "hypnosis as an exceptional concentrate of all the potentialities of mimesis."[25] And yet, once again, with the notable exception of Mikkel Borch-Jacobsen, the political implications of hypnotic/mimetic suggestion have not been at the forefront of mimetic theory so far. Donald Trump's television show, *The Apprentice*, provides us with a case study to join the insights of mimetic theory and crowd psychology. It also urges us to further mimetic theory by diagnosing how a reality *show* (fiction) paved the way for public identifications with an oppressive leader now at play in the sphere of *reality* shows as well (politics).

Chapter 2 takes a genealogical step back to the concept

of community that is entangled with fascist movements of the 1920s and 1930s in order to account for the emergence of the (new) fascist movements today. It does so by focusing on a heterogeneous thinker who has been celebrated as a precursor of a linguistic conception of the subject in the past century, but who can be productively aligned with mimetic theory in the present century: namely, Georges Bataille.

Like Girard after him, Bataille, in fact, develops a theory of the sacred that has violence and sacrifice at its starting point on the basis of anthropological hypotheses he shares with Girard. He also supplements mimetic theory by adding an explicitly political dimension to his diagnostic of what he calls "contagious," "affective" and "violent" modes of "sovereign communication" that introduce mimetic continuities between fascist leaders and their subjects.

Bataille is a strong theoretical ally to further new connections in mimetic theory. If he is now at the center of poststructuralist debates on community that are inoperative and *opposed to* fascism, mimetic theory reminds us that he developed a reflection on communal crowds that were operative and *attracted by* fascism. Heterogeneous fascist leaders like Hitler and Mussolini, he notices, rely not only on the power of hypnosis to cast a spell on the crowd, but also on accursed subject matters like sacrificial violence, sexual obscenity, and abject bodily matters that are paradoxically attractive due to their repulsive nature.

That such obscene matters are now the topic of daily news should urge us to take their power on the mimetic unconscious seriously. They trigger bodily reactions that might have been repressed in the past century yet are now fully manifest in the present century. They haunt a virtually dependent century that not only represents what Bataille calls our accursed share (*part maudite*) from a distance, but also disseminates its transgressive affective practices in the social and political world generating real pathologies. While the disciplinary focus in this chapter is different, my methodological assumption remains the same, or rather, double: my wager is that different disciplinary traditions like poststructuralism and mimetic theory that are usually split in competing and rivalrous camps should join forces to counter the fascist pathologies that are currently infecting our communities.

This balancing genealogical operation is a reminder that community, like the mimetic forms of "communication" that unite it, is a double-edged concept that can be put to both liberating and fascist uses. It also looks back to Bataille's account of fascist leaders who were "totally other" and generated movements of "attraction and repulsion" in past mimetic crowds in order to look ahead to the polarizing double effects new fascist leaders generate among contemporary, hypermimetic publics.

If chapters 1 and 2 focus on underdiscussed precursors of mimetic theory such as Le Bon, Tarde, and Bataille, chapter 3, "The Power of Myth Reloaded," leaps ahead to consider a dissident advocate of mimetic theory: the French philosopher Philippe Lacoue-Labarthe. Commonly associated with Jean-Luc Nancy and Jacques Derrida due to their work in common, it has not been sufficiently stressed that Lacoue-Labarthe was no less attentive to Girard in his career-long effort to "think or rethink *mimesis*."[26]

Unlike many of his generation, Lacoue-Labarthe took Girard's mimetic hypothesis seriously. While his most direct engagement with Girard appeared in "Typography," a silent, at times agonistic, but nonetheless thought-provoking conversation between the two authors traverses their entire oeuvres and will have to be traced in detail at some point. My genealogy here is confined to the problematic at hand. I thus focus on Lacoue-Labarthe's and Nancy's account of "The Nazi Myth" (1991), a seminal essay on the ontological and psychological foundations of fascism and Nazism. The two philosophers further the Platonic insight that an understanding of myth cannot be dissociated from the problematic of mimesis in general and affective contagion in particular.

Reframing Lacoue-Labarthe's and Nancy's account of the "Nazi myth" as a "mimetic instrument" in light of a broader tradition in mimetic theory is important for at least two reasons: first, the chapter provides a genealogical perspective that calls attention to the role of "collective mass emotions" in the formation of fascist myths that are currently being reenacted and reproduced; and second, it reveals how fascist leader figures (old and new) mobilize the dramatic skills of the actor along lines that are at least double, for they rely on the interplay of mimetic representations (Apollonian mimesis) and bodily impersonations (Dionysian mimesis) to make an impression on the crowd and public.

If, in the past, the tendency has been to restrict fascist forms of will to power to European leaders and the horrors they triggered, this genealogy calls attention to the interplay of visual and affective mimesis that is currently being disseminated via new media, threatening to escalate violence to what Girard, echoing Clausewitz, calls "extremes." Bringing this diagnostic to bear on the present, the last section returns to "the apprentice" with which we started in light of two conceptions of mimesis that are simultaneously at play in contemporary political fictions: if the creation of "alternative facts" have the power to generate appearances that dissolve the very notion of truth in yet another post (i.e., post-truth), they also induce an intoxicating state of mind that puts the critical faculties to sleep as it invites people to live in alternative fictional worlds—while phantom leaders take possession of the real world.

The book ends with a conversation around "Fascism, Now and Then" with political theorist William Connolly. Since the diagnostic that follows is directly entangled in the circumstances in which our paths crossed, both in the United States and in Europe, I would like to briefly relate them, in order to begin.

The Politics of Friendship

I had the privilege of meeting William (Bill) Connolly during a research stay that brought me back to the United States in 2013, when Barack Obama was still president. Having obtained a grant from Switzerland to pursue my research abroad, I chose Johns Hopkins University as a host institution for obvious and rather unoriginal genealogical reasons. René Girard, Jacques Derrida, and, more discretely, Philippe Lacoue-Labarthe had in fact left behind a strong legacy in mimetic theory, especially at the Humanities Center, where, at the invitation of Paola Marrati and Hent de Vries, I could pursue my research on mimesis.

But mimesis, I soon realized, was being discussed in other disciplines as well, in related departments like Anthropology and Political Science, for instance, albeit under different conceptual masks. I became aware of this synergy as Jane Bennett invited me to join a reading group over the summer of 2015. I immediately said yes, and it was in this informal group—Bataille would have called it an "elective community"—that I first met Bill Connolly.[27] We soon found a common interest in the work of Nietzsche, which, from different perspectives, led to shared concerns with a minor tradition of thought attentive to affect, contagion, mirror neurons, and the relation between literature and political theory, environmental studies and the neurosciences, all topics that we discussed in the reading group, graduate seminars, and numerous informal conversations.

The subjects of discussion were heterogeneous in nature, but as the 2016 presidential campaign started to pick up speed, we found ourselves increasingly preoccupied with Donald Trump's affective and infective rhetorical strategies. Coming at the problematic of the actor from different perspectives, we both sensed the mimetic and contagious power at play in this authoritarian type and took it seriously at a time in which his candidacy seemed mostly a subject for comedy.

My sense was that Connolly, whose engagement with a pluralist political tradition spans over forty years, was ideally placed to expose Donald Trump's affective strategies; and he did so in several incisive posts in a blog titled *The Contemporary Condition*.[28] At the time, I felt less confident in publicly expressing my political views. As a visitor with a precarious appointment, I chose the less courageous option of lying low. Still, within the safe confines of academia, I organized a conference titled "Poetics and Politics" in February 2016 that addressed the current becoming fictional of the political.[29]

Meanwhile, the eerie echoes of the rhetorical strategies I had analyzed in *The Phantom of the Ego* (2013), especially with respect to the mimetic communication between fascist leaders and crowds, kept amplifying in the theater of contemporary politics.

In a sense, I felt, once again, that this was not directly *my* problem. I was not a U.S. citizen, I was not in a position to vote anyway, and as Trump was gaining in popularity, my time at Johns Hopkins (and in the United States, for that matter) was speedily coming to an end. I was busy packing. Gunshots were intensifying in the neighborhood in Western

Baltimore where we lived. And both my spouse and I were ready to find another school for our kids, a decision strengthened by what the authorities of the public school our son attended called "an accident": a four-year-old child in my son's parallel class was killed that winter. The circumstances of his death doubled the shock. He had found a shotgun in his house. It was loaded. His dad, it later turned out, was a policeman. So yes, we were ready to move.

And yet, as I left Johns Hopkins in the summer of 2016, just in time to escape Trump's victory, in order to return to Europe (somewhat accidentally landing in Germany—academic lives are complicated), I felt that this was indeed still *my* problem, after all. In the sense that the problematic of affective *mimesis* continued to be central to the rise of (new) fascist movements that were not confined to one nation but had the disconcerting potential to cross national borders.

It felt important to join forces from a distance—first of all, out of sympathy and solidarity with my U.S. friends, colleagues, and students, but also because new fascist leaders had been gaining power in Europe as well. On his side, Connolly went on to teach a graduate seminar titled

"What Was/Is Fascism" in the spring of 2017; on my side, I obtained a research grant from the European Research Council to continue my work on imitative behavior with a project titled *"Homo Mimeticus."*[30] Still we maintained regular contact. Our thoughts moved back and forth in the weeks preceding the 2016 elections; we shared work in progress, found occasions to meet, and planned possibilities for collaboration. Fascist politics, in short, had fortified a politics of friendship.[31]

This conversation carried out in Weimar, Germany, in the summer of 2017 traces some of our shared concerns on issues as diverse as the rhetoric of fascism, mimetic contagion, political satire, the power of myth, and the dangers of new or aspirational fascism in the age of the Anthropocene. Needless to say, it is not meant as a conclusion but as a starting point for future theoretical reflections and, above all, political resistance.

1
Crowd Psychology Redux

The link between fascism's power of affection (or *pathos*) and mimetic behavior was once well-known at the dawn of the twentieth century. Imitation, in its conscious and, especially, unconscious manifestations, was then a popular subject of analysis. It concerned not only philosophy and psychology but also emerging human sciences (or *logoi*) such as sociology, anthropology, and especially crowd psychology, a discipline that provided a patho-*logical* account of the mimetic contagion that fascist leaders were quick to put to political use—and abuse.

And yet, as the phantom of fascism eventually dissolved in the second half of the twentieth century, the shadow of mimesis, and its legendary power to trigger affective contagion in the crowd, progressively fell to the background of the theoretical scene and, with few exceptions, was eventually relegated to an aberrant political anomaly that concerned only the few European countries who had openly embraced fascist governments, most notably Italy and Germany.

This theoretical neglect did not prevent mimesis from operating in political practices, though. Since humans remain, for better *and* worse, eminently mimetic creatures who are formed, informed, and transformed by dominant models, including political models, we should thus not be surprised to see that as tyrannical figures reappear in times of crisis, the shadow of mimesis—understood as an affective and infective force that leads people to mimic, often unconsciously, models—falls once again on the political scene.

A genealogical approach informed by past and present developments in mimetic theory can thus help us foreground a key trigger in the rise of (new) fascist movements that has been marginalized by mainstream social and political theories, but that is now, nolens volens, center stage in political practices: namely, the irrational trigger of mimetic contagion.

Much of what is currently at play in the process of becoming master of the actor does not sound completely new to mimetic theorists. From the pathological narcissism of mediatized leader figures to the mimetic desires of followers modeled on such figures, from violent rivalries with political adversaries to scapegoating mechanisms against minorities, from the readiness to sacrifice innocent victims (including children) to the potential escalation of nuclear wars that, more than ever, threaten to ensue as mirroring accusations between hypermilitarized governments are set in motion, the central mimetic mechanisms René Girard described can no longer be considered part of a theory of the violent origins of culture alone. Quite the contrary. In a mirroring inversion of perspectives, mimetic theory now directly informs political practices that, as Girard was quick to sense, are currently accelerating our violent progress toward potentially catastrophic destinations.[1]

The relevance of mimetic theory for catastrophic behavior has not gone unnoticed. Informed by the work of

René Girard but drawing explicitly on a tradition in crowd psychology that was attentive to mimetic contagion, the French theorist Jean-Pierre Dupuy has stressed the centrality of crowd behavior in situations of catastrophe. Drawing on Le Bon, Tarde, and especially Freud, Dupuy usefully reminds us that "the crowd is the privileged medium [*support*] for contagious phenomena."[2] He also offers a searching study of the "ambivalence" generated by the mimetic phenomenon of panic that is attentive to the process of "violent deindividu-alization" that dissolves the subject.[3] This double movement, as we shall see, operates not only in situations of panic. It is also constitutive of the ambivalent affects (new) fascist leaders generate in physical crowds and virtual publics during social and political conditions that may be momentarily experienced as "normal"—yet can lead to catastrophes in the long term.

There are thus ample reasons to justify a mimetic approach to authoritarian leaders that shadow fascist models, especially since (new) fascism, and the fluxes of affective contagion it generates, is still a largely unexplored area of investigation in mimetic theory. At the same time, mimetic theory is a growing, moving, and expanding field involved in a constant process of adaptation necessary to keep up with emerging mimetic pathologies that infect the present and future. There are thus other patho-*logical* reasons as well to convoke the register of mimesis.

For instance, it is well-known that fascist leaders, old and new, appeal to emotions rather than reason, *pathos* rather than *logos*, in order to generate an enthusiastic frenzy among potential voters assembled in what used to be called a "crowd." Robert Paxton, in his informed *The Anatomy of Fascism* (2004), goes as far as saying that "subterranean passions and emotions" function as fascism's "most important register"—and rightly so, for this register is contagious, and thus mimetic, and generates what Paxton calls "the emotional lava that set fascism's foundations."[4] These foundations, he continues, include the "sense of overwhelming crisis," "the belief that one group is a victim," the desire for a "purer community," the belief in "the superiority of the leader's instinct," "the beauty of violence," "the right of the chosen people to dominate others," among other distinctive symptoms that, he specifies, "belong more to the realm of visceral feelings than to the real of reasoned propositions."[5]

What we must add is that the contagious nature of

these feelings central to the subterranean foundations of fascism has been diagnosed in detail well before the rise of fascist movements. For instance, Friedrich Nietzsche is a philosopher who had the historical misfortune of having a nationalist, anti-Semitic sister who cast a political shadow on his legacy by implicating his name in the very fascist forces he denounced in his writings. Both Hitler and Mussolini presumably found a source of inspiration in Nietzsche's conception of the overman. And yet, if one takes the time to read Nietzsche, his virulent opposition to anti-Semitism, not to speak of German nationalism, should be clear enough.

Further, if one practices the art of reading as Nietzsche understands it—that is, as an art of "rumination"—then it soon becomes apparent that despite his fascination with forms of sovereign will to power, or rather because of it, he is one of the most insightful critics of mimetic pathos central to mobilizing the lava that flows through the channels of the psychology of fascism. Connecting the ancient philosophical concept of mimetic "pathos" with the modern psychological concept of "hypnosis," Nietzsche was among the first to diagnose the will to power of a "leader" (*Führer*) to cast a spell over the "masses" (*Massen*), which eventually led to massive submissions to the fascist ideologies he opposed, such as nationalism and anti-Semitism.[6]

Nietzsche was not alone in his diagnostic. The paradigm of hypnosis to account for mimetic contagion was in the air in fin-de-siècle Europe. Advocates of the newly founded discipline of crowd psychology, such as Gustave Le Bon and Gabriel Tarde, wanted to account for a psychological change that overcame people assembled in a crowd. Otherwise rational individuals, they observed, were suddenly easily affected by emotions—especially violent emotions that would spread contagiously, generating mimetic continuities between self and others. In their views, imitation and contagion could not easily be disentangled. As Le Bon puts it, in *Psychologie des foules* (1895), "in a crowd, every feeling, every act is contagious"; and he adds, "imitation, a phenomenon which is considered so influential on social behavior, is a simple effect of contagion."[7] Le Bon is here inverting Tarde's affirmation in *Les lois de l'imitation* (1890) that "all social similitude has imitation as a cause," an affective cause that triggers what he frenzied dispossessions have largely gone unnoticed on both side of the disciplinary divide.

The aloofness is reciprocal. If crowd psychology is usually not internal to the burgeoning field of mimetic theory, Girard is not mentioned in the most informed accounts of crowd psychology.[10] This mutual neglect is unfortunate, especially when the subject of investigation is a double mimetic phenomenon that emerges from the contagious interplay between the mimetic crowd and its (new) fascist leader. Hence the need to adopt a Janus-faced perspective that brings the insights of mimetic theory into closer collaboration with the insights of crowd psychology, and vice versa.

The reasons for building a bridge between these perspectives to cast light on the shadow of fascism are manifold, but let me at least mention a few general ones at the outset. First, historically, crowd psychology emerges in critical dialogue with human sciences such as sociology, anthropology, and psychoanalysis, which are equally central to mimetic theory. Second, both perspectives share an interest in challenging a solipsistic view of subjectivity in order to call attention to the relational, affective, and interpersonal power of mimetic affects. And third, both are in line with a theory of the unconscious that is not based on a repressive hypothesis but on a mimetic hypothesis instead. That is, a hypothesis that pays attention to an involuntary mirroring tendency to reproduce expressions and thoughts of others, especially dominant, authoritarian, and fascist others.

Let us look at this hypothesis more closely.[11]

The Age of the Crowd (Le Bon to Tarde)

The laws of imitation are psychological in nature, but crowd psychologists were quick to sense their direct political applications. Both Le Bon and Tarde, in fact, pointed out that "leaders" (*meneurs*) rely on mimetic laws in order to cast a spell on the psychic life of crowds. Comparing the power of leaders to the power of hypnotists, they drew from a psychological tradition that had hypnosis as a *via regia* to the unconscious in order to account for the fluxes of affective contagion that introduce collective sameness in place of individual difference. In particular, they relied on the notion of "suggestion" understood as a psychological propensity of crowds to unconsciously or semiconsciously mimic and assimilate ideas, opinions, and attitudes coming from others, especially respected, dominant, or prestigious others.

Crowd psychology, we should be prepared, does not hold up a flattering, narcissistic mirror to the psychic life of the ego in a crowd. It is perhaps also for this reason that, even in a post-Romantic period in which originality has been proved to be a *mensonge* (Girard's term), its major insights tend to be ignored. Le Bon summarizes the major psychological characteristics of the crowd thus:

> Dissolution of conscious personality, dominance of the unconscious personality, orientation by way of suggestion and contagion of feelings and ideas toward the same direction; tendency to transform suggested ideas immediately into actions: these are the principal characteristics of the individual who is part of a crowd. He is no longer himself but an automaton whose will no longer has the power to lead.[12]

Not only does an automaton lack the power to lead; he also desires to be led. This is, indeed, a troubling image not only for the mimetic psychology it presupposes but also, and above all, for the politics it can lead to. If we take this diagnostic of the mimetic crowd literally, the politics that ensues can in fact be potentially complicit with, rather than critical of, fascism.

The shadow of authoritarian politics haunts crowd psychology. Le Bon, for one, writing out of fear of the socialist masses, argued for the need of a prestigious leader or *meneur*, which, according to his conservative political agenda, was necessary to give the body politic a head. Considered from a political perspective, then, Le Bon is not the most obvious candidate to convoke in a *critique* of fascism, be it old or new—if only because his conservative politics, his fear of the specter of socialism (rather than of fascism), and above all, his openly racist, sexist, and classist assumptions of crowds as "feminine," "primitive," "savage," etc., did not withstand the test of history, contribute to the problem we are denouncing, and deserve to be diagnosed in terms of what I call a "mimetic pathology."[13] Le Bon will thus certainly not serve as our *political* guide in the critique of (new) fascism that follows.

And yet, at the same time, we should not hasten to throw out the baby of crowd psychology with the conservative political water in which it was born. Although the two are sometimes difficult to disentangle, the fact that we radically disagree with Le Bon's political conclusions does not mean that we should reject his mimetic insights. That both Mussolini and Hitler benefited from Le Bon's strategies to cast a spell on the crowd speaks against his politics but unfortunately also confirms his mimetic theory. Similarly, if Trump benefited from Girardian insights into the logic of mimesis, we should condemn its political use, but we have one more reason to take the theory seriously.[14] Crowds and scapegoats tend to go hand in hand, and (new) fascist leaders can be quick to learn the mimetic lesson. Hence we better catch up.

Genealogically speaking, crowd psychology paved the way and articulated laws of imitation that reach into the present. Le Bon, for instance, had identified distinctive rhetorical mechanisms that fascist leaders would soon use to trigger mimetic contagion in the crowd. They included, among other things, the power of repetition, the affective role of gestures and facial mimicry, the use of images rather than thoughts, of concise affirmations rather than rational explanations, the adoption of an authoritarian tone and posture—all of which, he specified, have the power to "impress the imaginations of crowds."[15] As he puts it: "The crowd being only impressed by excessive feelings, the orator who wants to seduce it must rely excessively on violent affirmations: exaggerating, affirming, repeating and never attempting to demonstrate anything through reason";[16] these are the strategies familiar to both orators and fascist leaders. Of particular importance, he also added, is the repetition of a simple nationalist "slogan" (say, a country made "great again") that unites the crowd, accompanied by a "captivating and clear image" (say, a "wall") that resolves a complex problem, as if by "magic."[17]

This diagnostic has not been popular in the second half of the past century, but unfortunately the rhetoric of fascism continues to cast a spell on the present century. It is thus perhaps useful to note that Le Bon was not alone

Again, the image is not flattering, but does it mean that it is false? It is actually shared by a number of influential theorists who do not explicitly work within the field of crowd psychology, yet further this tradition nonetheless. Elias Canetti, for instance, will define the crowd in terms of a "state of absolute equality," for "it is for the sake of this equality that people become a crowd"; but he also immediately adds, along lines that have clear political undertones: "Direction is essential for the continuing existence of the crowd. Its constant fear of disintegration means that it will accept *any* goal."[20] On a philosophical front, Hannah Arendt specifies: "Society is always prone to accept a person offhand for what he pretends to be, so that a crackpot posing as a genius always has a certain chance to be believed."[21] And she adds in terms that have not lost their validity but found ample confirmation in recent manifestations of self-proclaimed "stable geniuses" instead: "In modern society, with its characteristic lack of discerning judgment, this tendency is strengthened, so that someone who not only holds opinions but presents them in a tone of unshakable conviction will not so easily forfeit his prestige, no matter how many times he has been demonstrably wrong."[22]

A critical look at the contemporary political scene should be sufficient to prove the accuracy of such a diagnostic: we remain, indeed, eminently vulnerable to suggestion. It does not sound nice to say it, but crowd psychology urges us to consider that our ideas, emotions, opinions, and goals might not always be as original as they appear to be. They may at least be partially shaped mimetically, unconsciously, and hypnotically by the models or leaders that surround us. This is the reason why the mimetic unconscious is already a political unconscious. Its relational nature makes us vulnerable to all kinds of external influences, be they positive or negative, therapeutic or pathological, democratic or fascist.

Mimetic influences are especially visible in the crowd as subjects capitulate to fascist leaders who exploit the insights of crowd psychology to foster authoritarian regimes. But since fascist leaders grew out of mass support, we should not feel exempt from such mimetic influences in democratic countries as well. The spell of the word "democracy" is no protection for all kinds of mass-manipulations. As Jacob

Bernays recognized in *Propaganda* (1928): "The conscious and intelligent manipulation of the organized habits and opinions of the masses is an important element in democratic societies."[23] And capitalizing on crowd psychology, as well as on the insight that "politics was the first big business in America," Bernays sets out to explain how "the minority [i.e., the rich] has discovered a powerful help in influencing majorities [by] mold[ing] the mind of the masses [so] that they will throw their newly gained strength in the desired direction."[24] His book, which relied on Le Bon's and Tarde's theses, might be little read today in classes of critical theory, but his lessons in "public relations" are fully exploited in economic and political practices.

In the wake of the massive success of crowd psychology in the past, we can perhaps better understand why more recent social theorists have urged us to revisit this marginalized tradition. Serge Moscovici, for instance, in his informed account of crowd psychology, *The Age of the Crowd* (1985), finds it "astonishing that even today we believe that we can ignore its concepts and dispense with them."[25] His cautionary reminder is worth repeating: "At some time or another, every individual passively submits to the decisions of his chiefs and his superiors"; and he adds, in a mimetic mood, "the crowd is everyone, you, me, all of us."[26] More recently, Christian Borch ends his wide-ranging *The Politics of Crowds* (2012) with the realization that the "specter of crowds haunt[s] again sociological thought."[27] Borch also specifies that the "notion of suggestion, might prove more analytically useful than its bad reputation suggests."[28] What we must add is that this psychological notion remains especially useful if what is at stake is the politics of fascist crowds.

Suggestion and Desire (Freud to Girard)

Why is the reputation of suggestion bad? And if it was bad in the past century, is it worth reevaluating it for the present century? At first sight, fin-de-siècle statements about the suggestibility of crowds could indeed be seen as the product of a past generation of social theorists who relied on an old-fashioned and long disproved model of hypnosis to account for the power of leaders to influence the masses.

This view is much influenced by Sigmund Freud, who was himself a theorist of crowd behavior. In *Group Psychology and Analysis of the Ego* (1921), the father of psychoanalysis, in fact, dismissed suggestion as a "magical" concept that "explains everything [and] was itself to be exempt from explanation."[29] As I have outlined Freud's trial of hypnosis elsewhere, a brief summary must suffice here.[30]

Freud's diagnostic of what he called "crowd psychology" (*Massenpsychologie*) rests on the shoulders of the tradition we have just considered. In fact, he explicitly echoed Le Bon's and Tarde's question as he asked: "Why...do we invariably give way to this contagion when we are in a group?"[31] The answer, however, proved originally different. Freud, in fact, broke with the mimetic tradition that had suggestion as a main door to the unconscious by establishing a distinction between two "emotional ties" that bind the crowd to the leader, most notably "desire" and "identification"—or as Freud also puts it, wanting to *have* as opposed to wanting to *be* the other.[32]

Schematically put, Freud stretches his personal psychology to account for crowd psychology via three structurally related theoretical steps. First, he posits that "libido" or "love" (wanting to have) is what constitutes "the essence of the group mind" in the sense that members of the crowd love the leader, just as members of an army love their commander, and members of the Church love Christ. Second, he complicates this account by inserting a second emotional tie, namely, "identification" (wanting to be), by saying in a more recognizably mimetic language that "identification endeavours to mould a person's own ego after the fashion of the one that has been taken as a model." And finally, he triangulates these two emotional ties by stating that "identification is based on the possibility or *desire* of putting oneself in the same situation."[33] Desire, in other words, paves the way for identification; wanting to have what the model has leads to wanting to be the model.

But is it really so? Or is it the other way around? This is, indeed, Girard's question as he zeroes in on a structural ambivalence in Freud's account of social formation in *Violence and the Sacred* (1972), thereby aligning himself with the tradition of crowd psychology that concerns us. On the one hand, Girard points out that Freud posits the primacy of desire (or object cathexis) over identification (or mimesis); on the other hand, he also notices that Freud defines identification as "the earliest expression of an emotional tie with another person."[34] Which version is true? As Girard argued, "Freud saw that path of mimetic desire stretching out before him and deliberately turned aside."[35] In Girard's inversion of the Freudian model, then, it is because the subject of the crowd identifies with the model qua leader *first* that he or she ends up desiring what he desires. Hence, in his view, "the mimetic model directs the disciple's desire to a particular object by desiring it himself."[36] Mimesis, for Girard, is thus central not only to personal psychology, but to crowd psychology as well.

In the wake of Girard's reframing of Freud's account of crowd psychology, the problematic of identification has been amply discussed in mimetic theory. The connection with fascist politics has also been noticed, most notably by Mikkel Borch-Jacobsen, who in *The Freudian Subject* (1982) persuasively exposed the narcissistic nature of Freudian politics. As Borch-Jacobsen puts it toward the conclusion of a rigorous reading of *Group Psychology*: "The leader is a narcissistic object: the group members love *themselves* in him, they recognize him as their master because they recognize *themselves* in him."[37] Even without having read Freud, this dynamic of recognition should now be familiar. Mirroring reflections are all too visibly exploited by narcissistic leaders qua masters who turn this desire for recognition to new fascist uses.

But Borch-Jacobsen goes farther as he notices not only a narcissistic but also an authoritarian bent implicit in Freudian politics. As he puts it: "Like Gustave Le Bon, to whose analyses he owes more than he is ready to acknowledge, Freud places the chief at the beginning and the helm of the group, the Masse. . . . Only the chief (only the *Führer*, since that is how Freud translates Le Bon's *meneur*) assures the cohesion of that mass."[38] This is a serious objection that casts a shadow on psychoanalysis. For Borch-Jacobsen, in fact, Freudian politics, not unlike Le Bon's politics, is mimetic, narcissistic, and potentially fascist politics.

Again, this politics should be condemned for political reasons; yet this does not mean that the model of hypnotic suggestion Freud foreclosed in his account of the crowd for theoretical reasons has stopped operating on a massive scale. There are in fact at least two problems with Freud's avowed "resistance"[39] to the hypnotic tradition of the unconscious internal to crowd psychology—one historical, the other theoretical. Historical because, as I mentioned, both Hitler and Mussolini directly benefited from Le Bon's manual on how to cast a spell on the crowd, relying not only on the concept of "suggestion" but also on hypnotic practices like authoritarian affirmation, repetition, use of gestures and images, postponements of meetings in the evening in order to better induce hypnosis—mimetic techniques that, as William Connolly recently argued, are still effectively mobilized by aspirational fascist leaders who trigger "fascist contagion."[40] Theoretical because Freud never stopped being haunted by the riddle of suggestion, which, as Borch-Jacobsen demonstrated, continues to latently inform his notion of identification and transference.[41]

If we further these important historical/theoretical objections, a mimetic supplement is in order. While Freud denied the existence of a direct "sympathy" responsible for the affective "contagion" that spreads from self to others in a crowd,[42] Tarde affirmed the possibility of a type of "sympathy" or "unconscious imitation" based on what he called, on the shoulders of a physio-psychological diagnostic of the mimetic unconscious, "an innate tendency in the nervous system toward imitation."[43] Do I feel the *pathos* of the other directly, so that a mirroring *sym-pathos* ensues, or is a form of mediation or triangulation necessary? This riddle remained unresolved for a long time, but with the benefit of political and theoretical hindsight, we should now be in a position to adjudicate between these competing accounts of the unconscious that (new) fascist leaders have learned to manipulate.

Crowd psychologists relied on a psychological—or better, physio-psychological—conception of the mimetic unconscious that was much neglected in the past Freudian century but that is currently returning to the foreground in the twenty-first century. An important scientific discovery is in fact lending increasing support to the mimetic foundations of human behavior, including, albeit indirectly, collective, mass behavior. A group of Italian neuroscientists led by Giacomo Rizzolatti and Vittorio Gallese discovered in the 1990s so-called mirror neurons in macaque monkeys, with striking implications for understanding human behavior as well.

Mirror neurons are motor neurons, that is, neurons responsible for motion, that fire not only when we move but also at the sight of movements such as gestures and facial expressions performed by others. Thus, the mirror neuron system (MNS), as it is now called in humans, "triggers" in the subject the unconscious reflex of reproducing the gestures or expressions of others, generating mirroring effects that are not under the full control of consciousness and are in this sense un-conscious.[44] Since empirical evidence is currently supporting the pre-Freudian idea that there is, indeed, an innate tendency to imitate in the nervous system, a mimetic conception of the unconscious that had long been forgotten becomes strikingly relevant again.

This mimetic reproduction might not be fully conscious, but it is nonetheless useful to consciousness. Advocates of the mimetic unconscious like Nietzsche and Tarde, Pierre Janet or Georges Bataille had in fact already pointed out that such mirroring effects play a crucial role in nonverbal forms of mimetic communication that are central to subject formation. And neuroscientists are currently confirming the role of the MNS in "understanding" the actions and intentions of others on the basis of a relational conception of subjectivity in which the gestures and expressions of the other are immediately felt, and thus understood, by the ego. As Rizzolatti and Sinigaglia put it, the "primary" function of the "mirror neuron system" concerns their "role linked to understand the meaning of the actions of others."[45] According to this view, we don't understand others only through the mediation of our mind (though we certainly do that too). At a most basic level, we understand others through an "embodied simulation" that gives us an immediate access to the psychic life of the other.[46] Hence "understanding" is now considered one of the primary functions of mirror neurons.

And yet, the double lenses of mimetic theory and crowd psychology also provide an important genealogical reminder. Mirroring mechanisms that are not under the full control of rational consciousness can be linked to rationality and logical understanding, for sure, but can also provide a breeding ground for irrational misunderstandings, not to speak of deception, manipulation, and violence. (New) fascist leaders may thus not promote logical understanding in their political speeches, but they sure know how to make mirror neurons fire via gestures that trigger mimetic pathos.

Trump's rhetoric is, once again, a case in point. It should not be dismissed for its logical weakness but studied closely for its mimetic effectiveness. He does not simply report a political program from a rational distance. Rather, he aggressively embodies his role with affective pathos. And it is the pathos, the aggressive tonality, the mimicry, histrionics, the shouts, and the gestures that fire mirror neurons among members of the crowd. The masses at Trump's rallies are incredibly suggestible, not only because the crowd dynamic diminishes human rational faculties and increases the receptivity to what others feel (horizontal mimesis), but also because Trump relies on his skills as an actor, amplified by origins of mimetic theory with its most recent developments, there are plenty of reasons to take Trump's histrionics seriously. Why? Because the embodied, affective, and performative dimension of his mimetic speeches, mimicry, and gestures triggers mirroring effects that have an influence on what subjects feel and think. These subjects are already susceptible to being affected by mimesis, not only because of the mirroring structure of their brains, or solely because an identification with Trump was already in place, but also because being part of a crowd subjected to a prestigious leader already begins to dissolve the boundaries dividing self and others via a mode of contagious communication that amplifies the mirroring tendencies of *Homo mimeticus*.

Reframed in this real-life scenario, it is clear that mirror neurons are not only central to understanding. They are also effective in generating a mimetic pathos that is deprived of all logical understanding whatsoever—yet is politically effective in generating affective and infective pathologies nonetheless. This is not a new insight. A mimetic tradition that goes from Plato to Nietzsche, Bataille to Derrida, to Girard and beyond has continuously alerted us that mimesis is an ambivalent concept that cuts both ways, for it is the source of both insight and deception, therapies and infections, or to use our language, patho-*logies* and pathologies.

A diagnostic *logos* on the infective power of mimetic *pathos* is especially necessary if these mirroring mechanisms are not triggered within the organized structure of the lab in which scientists zero in on an ideal brain considered in isolation. Mirror neurons are, in fact, particularly active outside the lab as well, and tend to fire in collective situations that blur the boundaries between self and others and accentuate mimetic behavior. As crowd psychologists noted, recuperating an insight as old as Plato, in a crowd the subject is impressed by gestures, mimicry, and authoritative affirmations. The figure on the stage might be far from an ideal model, yet he triggers embodied reactions nonetheless.

What we must add is that the contemporary subject of the crowd is also continuously exposed to an affective contagion reloaded in the virtual sphere by what Gabriel Tarde called "the public." And if the crowd is suggestible to fascist messages, the public is suggestible to fascist uses of (new) media.

The Age of the Public

Supplementing Le Bon's claim that we live in the "age of the crowd," Gabriel Tarde replied at the dawn of the twentieth century that we are entering the "era of the public" (*ère du public*) in which contagion operates at a distance, inaugurating what he called the "social group of the future."[48] The public, for Tarde, is a crowd in which its members are not in direct physical contact. Rather, he says that the contact is purely "virtual" insofar as members of a public are exposed to a *mass* medium while being physically isolated. As Tarde puts it, they are held together by fluxes of mental "contagion without contact" (*contagion sans contact*) mediated by what he calls a "suggestion at a distance" (*suggestion à distance*).[49]

How does a mental suggestion contaminate from a distance? How can a pathos of *distance* turn into a *sym*-pathos (feeling with)? Tarde's answer is that the public's affective contagion is purely mental and is triggered by what he calls "the unconscious illusion that our feelings are shared with a great number of minds" who are reading the same information "simultaneously."[50] Simultaneity of exposure to a whether its *message* is true news or fake news. What matters is that the *medium* disseminates virtually shared, daily news.

Tarde's analysis of the ways mass media contribute to generating an unconscious mass opinion that could easily be manipulated from a distance was primarily focused on newspapers. While he considered publics more capable of reflection than crowds, he continued to worry that the "docile and gullible" reader remains easy prey to unconscious influences or suggestions. He also feared a shift in the quality of media in the transition from books to newspapers, which he summarized with the following formula: "It has been said that the man who reads a single book is to be feared; but what about the man who reads a single newspaper"—and he adds, self-critically: "This man is each one of us."[51]

Tarde did not live long enough to see a period in which not even a single newspaper is being read. What about the person who reads the news from a single Facebook or Twitter account? Is this person soon becoming each one of us? There lies the contemporary danger. And yet, Tarde's laws of imitation nonetheless continue to speak to present virtual publics and the somnambulism they generate. His anticipation of "fast communications" with the power to generate a "virtual crowd," which he prophetically designated as the "social group of the future," not only proved historically correct,[52] it also paved the way for more recent philosophical recuperations of the notion of crowd qua public.

Peter Sloterdijk, for instance, on the shoulders of Tarde, speaks of a society in which "one is a mass without seeing others,"[53] thereby recuperating Tarde's notion of public in order to account for a shift from a culture of leadership to one of entertainment. As he puts it, "The secret of the leader of that time and the celebrities of today consists in the fact that they resemble their dullest admirers more strongly than any person involved dares imagine."[54] Sloterdijk, it's worth noticing, did not have Donald Trump as an example to support his point. Since we do, we have even more reasons to take crowd psychology seriously.

Conversely, and in a more cynical view, Jean Baudrillard speaks of the "silence" cast on masses in postmodern societies in which "the masses have no opinion and information does not inform them."[55] Baudrillard recuperates the category of "mass" from the mimetic tradition that concerns us, and in many ways, his claim about the failure of information to inform mass opinion is a radicalization of Tarde's analyses. He also anticipates an age of generalized disinformation that currently goes under the rubric of "post-truth," an age that no longer rests on the logic of representation but is dominated by hyperreal simulations that have no connection with reality whatsoever. This proliferation of simulation leads to what he calls the death of the political, of the social, and of reality as such. As he puts it: "Models of simulation and imaginary referent for use by a phantom political class which now no longer knows what kind of 'power' it wields over it, the mass is at the same time the death, the end of this political process thought to rule over it."[56]

Baudrillard's point is well taken, but we should also specify that this phantom political class has materialized. Consequently, hyperreal simulations continue to produce mimetic effects rooted in the materiality of real life. Perhaps, then, the epistemic break between simulation and mimesis might not be as clear-cut as Baudrillard at times suggests. His provocative claim that "the only genuine problem is the silence of the mass, the silence of the silent majority"[57] who can no longer be represented, for it is alienated and has "imploded" as a black hole, does not fully account for the mimetic or, as I prefer to call it, hypermimetic circulation that allows for fictional shows to churn out apprentice presidents—and for mimetic voters to not so silently bring simulated yet nonetheless real presidents to power.

No matter how hyperreal the medium, there is an embodied materiality to mimesis that is hard to erase. Judging from the success of all kinds of actors with crowds and publics alike, it seems that we have never been more mimetic and vulnerable to hypnotic suggestion. This is indeed what Timothy Snyder recently suggests as he convokes the pre-Freudian language of "hypnosis" and "trance" in order to account for a "logic of the spectacle" in which "the two-dimensional world of the internet [is] more important than the three-dimensional world of human contact."[58] Perhaps we're even entering a new stage in the laws of imitation that blurs the line between hyperreal simulations and real mimesis, and which I propose to call hypermimesis.

Following the laws of imitation from the crowd to the public allowed us to stretch the analysis of mimetic behavior into a hypermimetic present in which hyperreal simulations have real, all too real mimetic effects. The age of virtual publics also confirms the Nietzschean diagnostic that figures like actors who are at home in the world of fiction are now in a better position to rely on all kinds of new media that blur the line between the private and the public, fiction and politics, truth and lies, hyperreal simulations and dramatic impersonations. What we still need to consider is that hypermimesis is central to mass identifications with new leaders who become popular via reality *shows* first, before becoming masters of that *reality* show par excellence that politics is currently becoming.

To Have or to Be? Trumping the Question

If we now return to the present on the joint shoulders of mimetic theory and crowd psychology, it is apparent that mimetic communication played a key role in Donald Trump's election and is likely to remain center stage in the rise of new fascist leaders. In addition to Trump's embodiment of traditional features of the American Dream (most notably his wealth, be it real or, more realistically, fictional), his mediatized persona staged in TV shows like *The Apprentice* is also likely to have amplified his power of mimetic fascination in the sphere of fiction among the *public* first, thereby paving the way for his political success in the *crowd* of supporters as well.

As Umberto Eco was quick to warn us in his account of "Ur-fascism," in an age in which fascist leaders can take over old and new media like the television and the Internet, "we must be ready to identify other kinds of Newspeak, even if they take the apparently innocent form of a popular talk show."[59] Popular reality shows hosted by soon-to-be apprentice presidents are particularly insidious and dangerous, for they already blur the line between reality and fiction and pave the way for turning the political itself into a fiction.[60]

Since this hypermimetic interplay between fiction and politics, public and crowds, real imitations and hyperreal simulations is indeed central to the rise of new fascist leaders, in guise of conclusion let us take Eco's warning seriously and put mimetic theory to the test in the sphere of a mimetic fiction first in order to see if the psychoanalytical distinctions between identification and desire, wanting to have and wanting to be, apply to hypermimetic politics as well.

In *The Apprentice*, mimesis is center stage, for identification is at least double as it operates both inside the show and outside, in the real world. Inside the show, the carefully selected candidates that tightly fit normative standards of beauty and conform to aggressive neoliberal values (radical individualism, ruthless ambition, competitive rivalry, etc.) serve as models that attract identification of viewers outside the show as well. Spectators of *The Apprentice* must in fact have a desire to be (like) the potential apprentices and, as in all agonistic contests, are likely to identify with one of the two competing teams.

And yet, since these competing candidates are themselves subjects motivated by the desire to be a successful businessperson, of which Trump sets himself up as an ideal, a hierarchy of models is already in place that situates spectators at two removes from the ideal model. The mimetic logic is simple, hierarchical, and effective: spectators identify with the apprentices who identify with the master. From such a distance, the spectators' mimetic pathos is first and foremost shared with the apprentice candidates and their efforts to fulfill a given business-related task.

This identification, however, is limited; it usually lasts until the much-coveted spectacle at the culmination of each episode. As the losing team needs to face the boardroom chaired by Trump and often including his family members, in order to account for their failure, a predictable mimetic and quasi-sacrificial turn ensues: the members of the team usually gang up against a single victim and designate a scapegoat. Responsibility for violence is thus structurally located within the mimetic team, thereby clearing the way for the sacrificer, in all good conscience, to point his finger and pull the trigger of his notorious symbolic execution expressed with pathos: "You're fired!"

The desire of the candidate to become an apprentice millionaire in a materialist-oriented culture that promotes models like Trump is of course not original; it is dictated by real and fictional models that are already pervasive in the culture and are visibly at play in shows like *The Apprentice*.

That this desire leads to rivalry, not with the mediator as such, who remains at the superior level of what Girard calls "external mediation,"[61] but with the other members of the "team" is equally inevitable given the rivalrous dimensions of the show based on a process of progressive elimination itself modeled on the competitive structure of neoliberal capitalism. Hence, the need for a violent exclusion—often via aggressive and pitiless accusations that designate the so-called weakest member of the team—already emerges from within the rivalrous community.

It's a basic and rather crude strategy of survival that allows the firing to be directed against what Girard calls a "single victim [that] can be substituted for all the potential victims."[62] That spectators enjoy watching such a show is itself confirmation of the public appeal of violence in which one or more victims are "fired" allowing the other members of the "team" to continue the show—at least until the next ritual firing takes place. The dynamic perfectly conforms to the Girardian schema: the desire for the same object inevitably leads to rivalry, violence, and ultimately sacrifice as a cathartic resolution for the spectator to enjoy at a distance.

It is in fact difficult to find a clearer and more condensed illustration of Girard's theory.

But, we may also wonder, who is the "you" who is being "fired" here? And why should we identify with the sacrificer in the first place? Here the mimetic dynamic is less clear. But if we are right in assuming that in a mass-mediatized culture the division between the new media and mass behavior is not clear-cut, it might have played a major role in Trump's political victory nonetheless. Let's take a closer diagnostic look.

Within the show, the victim is the fired apprentice, of course. But if we happened to identify with his/her position—unless one is writing on Trump, why watch the show otherwise?—there is a psychic side of the public that vicariously experiences being fired as well. The finger/gun pointing at the failed apprentice framed in a medium shot that breaks the fourth wall comes close to pointing to us as well; and as the apprentice's dreams of success fail within the reality show, so do ours—at one remove from the show, in real life.

This dynamic is, in a sense, not new. As Georges Bataille

recognized, this is after all the shared function of both sacrificial and tragic "spectacles": we experience death, physical or symbolic, via the "subterfuge" of a sacrificial victim—real or fictional—who "dies" in our place. Tragedies, novels, movies, and now reality shows offer repeated occasions for these vicarious sacrificial experiences Bataille groups under the rubric of "spectacle."[63] As he puts it: "It is a question, at least in tragedy, of identification with a character that dies and of believing that we die, while remaining alive."[64] And since we are not seriously affected by this death, Bataille specifies: "But it's a comedy!"[65] Thus, Bataille concludes: "Man does not live by bread alone but by comedies through which he voluntarily deceives himself."[66] Needless to say, a mass-mediatized culture exploits this need for daily deceptions. Judging from the success of such sacrificial shows, they have become our daily bread.

These deceptions are certainly at play in all kinds of spectacles with a mass appeal. But what if we live in ages in which comedies have dramatic political effects in real life as well? If we don't let go of this hypermimetic dynamic, we notice that after the firing, spectators' identificatory allegiances inevitably shift from the now (symbolically) dead apprentice qua sacrificial victim toward the narcissistic business model qua sacrificer. An interesting mimetic shift from the (failed) apprentice to the (ideal) model has thus just taken place that cuts across the distinction between show and reality.

The show, in other words, is not about the apprentice; it is about the master. Trump is visibly the original narcissistic model the apprentice is supposed to mimic within the real-ity *show*. At one remove, in *reality*, spectators may initially identify with the sacrificial apprentice, until the firing devalues the apprentice and glorifies the power of Trump. Put in more classical terms, identification with Trump is a dramatic effect of the tragic structure (or *muthos*) of this show. Hence a perverse desire to be Trump, to identify with the sacrificer rather than the victim is automatically triggered by the mimetic plot of the show every time that a firing takes place, generating mimetic pathos. Whether it generates the catharsis of tragic emotions like pity and fear, is uncertain, but it certainly generates a contagious demand for more pathos.[67] The show ran for fifteen seasons; it was still ongoing at the time Trump decided to enter another reality television show and run for the presidency.

We were wondering why the victim identifies with the oppressor, not only in reality shows but also in political fictions. *The Apprentice* illustrates a perverse hypermimetic dynamic that is now at play in political spectacles as well. In their social *reality*, the working-class voters who supported Trump are actually on the side of the sacrificial victims. Living in miserable social conditions, deprived of basic social services, not sustained by unions, driven by fear of others, and subjected to real forms of deprivation that render their lives precarious, they are not likely to fire anyone anytime soon in real life—but can always potentially be fired instead. And, paradoxically, for this reason they are deeply impressed by the power they lack and wish to have.

This mimetic paradox is then aggravated by an increasingly mediatized political world modeled on a form of aggressive, rivalrous, and violent entertainment in which it is becoming increasingly difficult—Bataille would say impossible—to distinguish between life and fiction, the show and the reality, especially in a population who has been deprived of a solid education in the humanities central for the development of critical thought. Hence, if members of a public have already identified with Trump in a mass-mediatized fictional reality *show*, they are also likely to identify with him in an equally mediatized political *reality* show; if they enjoyed a violent rhetoric within the show, they are likely to enjoy the same rhetoric in real life; if they were suggestible as a public they are likely to have their suggestibility amplified in a crowd.

The fact that the medium remains the same in the shift from entertainment to politics, and that politics is itself modeled on entertainment, confuses the reality and the show, politics and fiction. Hence as politics is experienced as a fiction, politicians are evaluated according to their dramatic performance—rather than their political message. Spectators of the reality show at Trump's rallies might thus have aesthetic rather than political criteria in mind as their mimetic unconscious might lead them to ask: Could I identify with the protagonist? Did he make me feel good? Or if I feel far from good, did his accusations and denigrations at least make me feel better—and others worse? Above all, would I want to watch this show on television again tomorrow? And as I think of the next show, doesn't America already begin to feel great again?

True, these are questions that pertain to a reality *show*; but since the show has become reality, is it so unlikely that they are now used to rate political spectacles as well? My point is that on top of what Trump represents in a culture already driven by having rather than being, what seems rather than what is, shows like *The Apprentice* paved the way for the election of an apprentice president in real life. And this is a tragedy!

Was the desire to be Trump triggered by what he has, or is it the other way around? If Freud argued that desire for an "object" (his term for a woman, most notably the mother) precedes identification with a model qua father figure, and Girard, in a mirroring inversion of perspectives, stressed that identification with the model actually directs the desire toward the object, the case of Trump blurs the line between these two distinct "emotional ties" insofar as both the desire to be and to have are simultaneously constitutive of the mimetic *pathos* he triggers.

As the name capitalized on his towers makes visible for all to see, Trump is indeed the name of both a subject and an object—the fake-golden brand plastered on objects being so constitutive of the subject that it cannot be dissociated from what he "is." Spectators qua voters who identify with Trump do so because of what he has, which already defines what he is, and who/what they would like to be/have as well. From Trump Tower to Trump Golf Courses, Trump Casinos to Trump Beauty Pageants, Trump Wine to Trump Steaks, to whatever other "objects" he owns, an untidy intermixture of wanting to be and wanting to have is at play in the mimetic *pathos* that ties Trump to his crowd of supporters, trumping the fundamental distinction on which Freud's account of mass psychology rests.

As the pre-Freudian tradition of crowd psychology suggested, then, the case of Trump indicates that both wanting to have and wanting to be are at play in emerging forms of suggestibility that rest on the interplay between the public and the crowd. While (new) fascist leaders will continue to rely on collective mass emotions in order to rise to power, counting on the mirroring reflexes that lead humans to affectively respond to all the strategies of the actors, these actors turned masters can at the same time rely on new media in order to cast a more ramified spell on the public that will in turn accentuate suggestibility in the crowd. In this process of spiraling circulation, the distinction between reality and show, fiction and politics, but also truth and lies, origin and copy, hyperreal simulation and embodied imitation, becomes part of a hypermimetic dynamic that thrives on simulations that may appear comic from a virtual distance, yet trigger political tragedies in real life.

Despite the innovation in the medium, then, the old concept of mimesis remains strikingly relevant to account for the unconscious influences that are currently at play on new social media. What the case of Trump teaches us is that hypermimetic media can easily be hijacked by actors—all kinds of actors who turn out to be themselves puppets whose strings are pulled by foreign oligarchic and quite hostile powers. Together, it is becoming increasingly clear that these new media contribute to spreading fascist messages among an increasingly disinformed public vulnerable to contagious pathologies.

All countries, I'm afraid, are vulnerable to hypermimesis and the (new) fascism it disseminates. It is thus urgent for mimetic theory to further develop critical patho-*logies* to diagnose and, perhaps, rechannel communal movements as well.

2

The Mimetic Community

Why has a concept that belonged, a few decades ago, to the margins of philosophy become such a central topic of theoretical investigation in recent years? Over the last three decades we have in fact heard of communities that are "imagined" and "real," "inoperative" and "cooperative," "unavowed" and "disavowed," "conflagrated" and yet "to come"; we have even heard of communities "laughing" and, more recently, "growling."[1] The echoes are strong, and the growing number of books on the subject of community testifies to the productivity, timeliness, and, above all, streaming force of a concept that is currently gathering speed and momentum, generating what Jean-Luc Nancy calls "a subterranean torrent that passes underneath, making everything tremble."[2]

The experience of community is, indeed, traversed by affective flows that are eminently contagious, are commonly shared, and generate contradictory effects that have the power to make the body politic tremble. Yet, in order to reframe this concept in light of the recent political resurgence of communal movements that make us tremble, it is important to recall that community is first and foremost a philosophical concept rooted in an untimely mimetic tradition that has been somewhat neglected in recent accounts, but continues to direct these movements' theoretical and political destinations—albeit in invisible, subterraneous, yet no less powerful ways.

Genealogy of Community

Shifting focus from the negative conceptions of crowds dominant in the 1890s to the more positive, yet equally destabilizing concept of community that re-emerged nearly a century later, in the 1980s, this chapter retraces some of the conceptual and affective sources of this torrential tradition, and begins in the proximity of the beginning. That is, by articulating a necessarily partial genealogy of key theoretical figures that first channeled the problematic of community in the twentieth century, contributing to generating affective torrents that—for better, but also for worse—now flow into the twenty-first century as well.

My hypothesis in this chapter is that looking back to theorists of community like Nancy, but also Maurice Blanchot and, especially, Georges Bataille, a thinker whose investigations on the destabilizing interplay of crowds and communities anticipated powerful insights into violent and sacred forms of communication later developed by mimetic theory, is urgent today for at least two reasons.

First, these heterogeneous theorists in general, and Bataille in particular, foreground, in their singular voices, the experiential foundations of community on the basis of a mimetic conception of sovereign communication that has remained in the shadows so far, yet paves the way for political phantoms to come. As Nietzsche was among the first to recognize, mimesis has the power to turn the ego into what he calls a "phantom of the ego" (*Phantom von Ego*),[3] thereby providing an untimely answer to Nancy's influential question at the twilight of the twentieth century: namely, "who comes after the subject?"[4]

Now that we are past the dawn of the twenty-first century, and all kinds of phantoms with the power to generate communal movements have appeared on the political scene, we need to go further and ask a related but different question: namely, what comes after community? According to Nancy, what is left are mere "phantasms of the lost community."[5] I suggest that after phantoms have taken possession of the lost community, the *mimetic community* remains.

And second, genealogical lenses reveal that the phantoms of past communities might help us diagnose the contagious dimension of present communal movements that are strikingly reminiscent of crowd movements we encountered in the preceding chapter. In particular, looking back to the foundations of mimetic communities in affective and infective experiences that took possession of entire crowds in the 1920s and 1930s in Europe makes us see that what Bataille calls "communal movements" of "attraction and repulsion" generate turbulent currents that can flow in quite opposite political directions—if only because they can be put to *both* revolutionary *and* fascist use.

The connections between fascist psychology and behavioral mimesis are manifold, historically rooted, and urgent to investigate. A genealogy of community that traces the origins of this concept back to Bataille's early concerns with what he called "The Psychological Structure of Fascism" shall bring us full circle, back to the present whereby we started. We shall thus move from an experience of revolt in which "people growl in common"[6] to a mimetic growl in which the revolting experience of (new) fascism itself is rendered common.

The spiraling circularity of these communal movements indicates that the mimetic community goes beyond good and evil. Hence the need to be as attentive to the conceptual side of community that already informs revolts in critical theory as to the affective side that always threatens to infect political practices. Nancy recently reminds us that in the 1980s, the "word 'community' reemerged as a sign of unease."[7] And in light of "battles," which, as Girard foresaw in his last major work, threaten to "escalate to extremes,"[8] this unease has only been growing since. My wager is that a genealogical approach that looks back to past and largely neglected precursors of community allows us to better see the mimetic efficacy of common, all too common political practices that we are now experiencing as well.

The most recent books on the subject of community open up new lines of investigations for the future; yet it is important to recall that the most influential thinkers who reopened the dossier on community in the 1980s started by looking back to the past. Nancy's and Blanchot's initial ambitions were much more limited than their most important precursors. They did not aim to uncover a distant, mythic past that posits the theoretical existence of homogeneous, organic, or sacrificial communities at the origins of culture, as sociologists (Ferdinand Tönnies), psychoanalysts (Sigmund Freud), and more recently, mimetic theorists (René Girard) affirmed[9]—though we will see that the problematic of ritual sacrifice and its dramatic reenactment in what these figures grouped under the rubric of the "sacred" or "myth" will continue to haunt mimetic theorists' historical concerns with contemporary fictions of the political.

Rather, thinkers of community looked back to a more recent historical, yet not less violent past in which, during some turbulent years in the 1920s and 1930s, heterogeneous communities were first and foremost experienced in political practice before being the object of communal inquiries in critical theory. This starting point is thus historical rather than mythic. It is not based on tragic fictions far removed from the original crisis, but zoom in on a real political crisis; it does not take its starting point from a theory of sameness but from a theory of difference. And yet, while being apparently far removed from some of the foundational hypotheses of mimetic theory, it provides a confirmation that mimesis and all it entails (affective contagion, hypnotic suggestion, sacrificial violence, etc.) is at the center of the crisis of modern politics, a mimetic crisis that now casts a shadow on contemporary politics as well.

But let us start from present accounts of community that hark back to an accursed precursor of mimetic theory.

An Accursed Precursor

Jean-Luc Nancy's *The Inoperative Community* (1986) occupies a privileged position in the genealogy of texts that relaunched discourses of community on the theoretical scene; and the recent echoes mentioned at the outset testify to the productivity, timeliness, and streaming force of his communal meditations in the twenty-first century as well.

Nancy is the first and most influential thinker who, in the wake of the failure of communism, reopened the dossier on community in the 1980s. And yet, he is careful not to posit his book as an origin. The adjective "inoperative" (*désoeuvrée*), for instance, is directly indebted to Maurice Blanchot, who, in turn, immediately replied to Nancy's first article on community in the journal *Aléa* (1983). And as Nancy is caught in a mimetic spiral that will lead him to reply thirty years later, in *The Disavowed Community* (2014), to Blanchot's reply, after the latter's death, it is crucial to remember that this infinite conversation, or *entretien infini*, is firmly rooted in a genealogical precursor who serves, if not as a model, at least as a common or, rather, shared interlocutor. If only because Nancy says that *The Inoperative Community* is first and foremost "an attempt to communicate with his experience."[10] His name, you will have guessed, is Georges Bataille.

To this day, Bataille remains an unclassifiable heterogeneous thinker who does not fit unilateral identifications. Roland Barthes's interrogations in the wake of the rediscovery of this untimely figure in the 1970s remain perfectly timely today: "How do you classify a writer like Georges Bataille? Novelist, poet, essayist, economist, philosopher, mystic? The answer is so difficult that the literary manuals generally prefer to forget about Bataille."[11] The difficulty has not diminished since. Quite the contrary. In a hyperspecialized academic world, it is becoming increasingly easy to forget a figure that escapes disciplinary categorizations.

An additional complication for the transdisciplinary field of mimetic theory is that those who actually did not forget about Bataille tended to align him with a philosophical concern with difference rather than sameness. Figures like Jacques Derrida, Michel Foucault, Jean Baudrillard, and more recently Jean-Luc Nancy, in fact, found in Bataille a precursor of their own heterogeneous thought and hastened to align him with a metaphysics of linguistic difference, discursive mediation, and ontological discontinuity. It is perhaps for this historical reason that Girard has generally tended to keep at a distance from what he called Bataille's "decadent estheticism."[12] And this distance was maintained despite the latter's concern with affective sameness, bodily immediacy, and ontological continuity—what Bataille also famously called the "continuity of being."[13]

Genealogical lenses have alerted us to a specific double movement at play in thinkers of mimesis. We should not be distracted by superficial oppositions, for theoretical distance often indicates that a shared mimetic *pathos* is already secretly but fundamentally at play in a communal *logos*. Among twentieth-century theorists, in fact, Girard is arguably the thinker who came closest to furthering Bataille's "general view of human life"[14] based on the anthropological hypothesis that sacrificial violence is at the origins of what he, Bataille, called "the sacred." As Lacoue-Labarthe also recognized, Bataille "continually underlies the Girardian problematic."[15]

This genealogical continuity is not accidental. Bataille developed his theory of the sacred in the 1930s and 1940s on the basis of philosophical (Kojève and Nietzsche), psychological (Freud and Lacan), as well as anthropological (Mauss and Durkheim) influences that would continue to inform Girard's take on violence and the sacred in the 1970s and 1980s. These shared preoccupations include topics such as desire and erotism, identification and contagion, religion and sacrifice, transgression and taboo, all categories that Bataille grouped under the general anthropological category of "sovereign communication" and the sacrificial violence it entails.

There are thus plenty of reasons for establishing a bridge between Bataille and mimetic theory, especially since Girard himself, in a passing and apparently dismissive remark that introduced a distance from Bataille, specifies: "On occasion Bataille is able to ... explain quite simply" that "the prohibition eliminates violence, and our violent impulses ... destroy our inner calm, without which human consciousness cannot exist."[16] Girard is thus ready to acknowledge that despite his aesthetic tendency to transgress prohibitions, Bataille is far from being an advocate of violence for its own sake and recognizes the necessity for peace.

Having foregrounded the general value of Bataille's thought for mimetic theory elsewhere, I hereby further the hypothesis that Bataille can serve as an "important supplement"[17] to Girard by adopting a specific genealogical perspective on a subject largely left in the shadows of mimetic theory so far: namely, the formation of fascist communities. This involves joining two areas of investigation that have tended to remain split in different camps in the past, yet might need to be thought in conjunction in the future.

The goal of this genealogy of community is threefold. First, it aims to contribute to rescuing Bataille from theoretical forgetfulness by stressing his centrality in contemporary discourses on community; second, it aligns Bataille with patho-*logical* concerns with mimetic sameness that have remained at the margins of philosophies of difference but are central to mimetic theory; and third, it aims to show that stepping back to Bataille's mimetic theory of community will allow us to leap ahead to the rise of (new) fascist communities. But let us proceed in order.

The Experience of Community

The forgetfulness about Bataille continues to this day in the wake of the massive dissemination of theories of community that usually mention his name only to relegate his thought once again, to the margins of philosophy.[18] This is surprising, since Nancy places Bataille, if not at the center, at least at the forefront of discourses on community. He states, for instance, in *The Inoperative Community*: "No doubt Bataille has gone farthest into the crucial experience of the modern destiny of community,"[19] or, "Bataille is without doubt the one who experienced first, or most acutely, the modern experience of community."[20] For anyone seriously concerned with the theoretical destiny of community, then, the question becomes: Who was the subject of this so-called crucial communal experience? And why does Nancy, just like Blanchot, take Bataille as a starting point to "indicate" what he calls, in a mimetic mode, "an experience—not, perhaps, an experience that we have, *but an experience that makes us be*"?[21]

Experience, subject, and being are concepts with a heavy philosophical past, to say the least. Still, it is important to notice at the outset that they are used otherwise in Nancy's Bataillean account of community. The subject of this communal experience is, strictly speaking, not a subject in the ordinary metaphysical sense of an autonomous, monadic, unitary, and rational being that exists independently of others. Nor is it a subject in the existential sense that posits that existence—and the choices it entails—precedes essence, for even this subject ultimately remains indebted to a classical *subjectum* that posits itself at a phenomenological distance from others. Rather, this is a subject that is, strictly speaking, not one, but plural instead. Nancy will later call it "singular-plural."[22]

Plurality, for Nancy, is already internal to singularity, for this subject is always permeable to the experience of others. Or, rather, this experience emerges in a relation of shared communication with others that are not simply exterior but are interior to one's being, generating what Bataille calls in *On Nietzsche* a "plural-singular being."[23] Hence Nancy says that community "is not the space of the *egos*—subjects and substances that are at bottom immortal—but of the I's who are always others,"[24] that is, "singular-plural" beings. While the emphasis often falls on plurality and difference rather than singularity and sameness, the communicative interplay between being singular and becoming plural cannot be easily dissociated from the heterogeneous experience of mimesis.

The concept Nancy uses to designate this shared experiential "space" at the heart of a community of plural-singular beings, and the movement of union and division this experience entails, is well-chosen. He calls it "sharing" (*partage*), a Janus-faced concept that captures, in a single stroke, the syncopated movement of attraction and repulsion, affective pathos and critical distance, division and sharing (Italians say *con-diviso*, shared divided; Germans speak of *mit-teilen*) that, for Bataille and, in a different but related sense, Nancy, is at the origins of the (dis)appearance of community. The subject of community, then, is located in between singularity and plurality, for it comes into being via an experience of shared communication that paradoxically *both* unites *and* divides, *con-divides* the singular ego with/from plural others.

As this preliminary theoretical frame suggests, Nancy's account of *partage*, which leads a singular-plural subject to both intimately partake in the experience of the other and

preoccupations. As Girard puts it: "The expulsion of the accursed share he [Bataille] talks about is nothing but a form of victimary mechanism,"[28] which also means that for both authors the sacred is bound up with violence. They also agree that sovereign/sacred experiences trigger an affective frenzy that brings the community together in fluxes of contagious effusions that introduce collective continuities in place of personal discontinuities. Bataille calls it "continuity of being," Girard calls it "crisis of difference," but the mimetic experience they refer to is essentially the same.

What Bataille adds is an inner, subjective dimension to this experience that includes desire but also stretches to encompass all kinds of heterogeneous affects that generate what he calls "gay contagion (*heureuse contagion*)."[29] Bataille will stress that in post-sacred societies this sovereign experience of community will be reenacted by free spirits like artists and lovers who refuse to be put to work, do not belong to any useful project that can be accomplished in time, and are thus, as he says in a famous letter to Alexandre Kojève, "unemployable" but also "unemployed," that is, out of work—"*sans emploi.*"[30] It is this useless quality of the sacred that cannot be put to any use, including a cathartic, unifying social use, that Bataille urges us to consider.

From inner experience to sacrifice, ecstasy to eroticism, laughter to tears, comedy to tragedy, communication to community, the trajectory of Bataille's entire thought brings the unemployed subject as close as possible to the limit experience of death, while retaining communication on the side of life. Thus, in his most influential book, *Inner Experience* (1943), which provides the ontological foundations for Bataille's theory of mimetic communication that will inform poststructuralist accounts of community, he writes that communication is "laughter, vertigo, nausea, loss of the self until death."[31]

The experience of communication is thus not restricted to a meaningful linguistic exchange but involves an intense affective contagion that cuts both ways: on one side, it flows through the "open wound" that swings the general economy of Bataille's communal thought to the side of a *pathos* he experiences with privileged others (friends, lovers, or as he calls them, *socii*) in real life; on the other, more philosophical side, he acknowledges a *distance* that is impossible to fully bridge, or transgress. Thus, he specifies: "As long as I live, I content myself with a back-and-forth, with a compromise."[32] This oscillating compromise generates an impossible type of sharing that Bataille aptly calls "*sans partage*"[33]—a phrase that cuts both ways, for it could mean without sharing but also sharing completely, or as Bataille would put it, without reserve.[34]

The experience of *partage*, then, applies to sovereign forms of communication like death, but also stretches to include sacrifice, ecstasy, laughter, and eroticism, thereby animating the plural experiences that inform Bataille's singular conception of community. Hence, what Bataille says at the opening of *Erotism* (1957) applies to community as well: "Eroticism, it may be said, is assenting to life up to the point of death."[35] Alternatively, as Bataille writes that "it is necessary for communal life to maintain itself at a level *equal to death*," or that "community cannot last except at the level of the intensity of death,"[36] he does so on the basis of an experience he calls inner; yet he paradoxically exposes the subject to the outside, generating a double movement of attraction and repulsion, or *partage*, that remains a structural constant in Bataille's inconstant meditations on community, and, as we will see, still captures the double movement generated by new phantoms of fascist communities.

The emphasis on the experience of death that can(not) be shared suffices alone to reveal that Bataille casts a long shadow on contemporary discourses on community. When Nancy writes, for instance, that "death itself is the true community of I's that are not egos,"[37] or when Blanchot echoes that "death is itself the true community of mortal beings,"[38] or, more recently, when Hillis Miller repeats that "community is defined by the imminence of death,"[39] as they do so, these theorists open up new theoretical perspectives for the future. Still, genealogical lenses reveal that despite their differential moves, they remain fundamentally inscribed in a Bataillean genealogy that looks back to violent and *sacred* rituals in order to better understand the resurgence of communal, *political* rituals.

Death is, indeed, an obsessive leitmotif in Bataille's thought and punctuates his most important works where the question of community is at play, from *Acéphale* to *The College of Sociology*, *Inner Experience* to *Guilty*, *On Nietzsche* to *Erotism*. And yet, if we want to reach the affective, contagious, or better, mimetic sources of Bataille's communal experience, it is important to specify that death is not the only horizon of community in Bataille's thought. Nancy's emphasis on the impossible experience of death, and the withdrawal of community it entails, is faithful to Bataille's conception of *ek-stasis* (and Heidegger's *Ek-sistence* and the conception of Being-with, or *Mitsein*, it embryonically entails), but he also leaves open an alternative Bataillean door to communal thinking that emphasizes (with Nietzsche) the importance of birth, contagious affects, and fluxes of life in the constitution and dissolution of what is in common. Nancy thus says that it is "birth" just as much as "death" that is the source of communication, and specifies that "only the community can present me my birth."[40] Similarly, in his reply to Nancy, Blanchot does not hide a "reservation" with respect to Nancy's reading of Bataille, yet he shares his insight that both "birth and death," "the first and last event . . . founds community."[41]

Community is thus defined not only by the impossible experience of death, but also, and for us more important, of Bataille's "elective communities" qua "secret societies,"[43] due to the mystery that surrounds it. I note in passing that Acéphale was radically opposed to established forms of community (church, state, nation, etc.); the headless body André Masson drew for the cover of the journal with the same name is a mythic figure that expresses what Bataille calls "sovereignty destined to destruction."[44] In the mid-1930s, Bataille is thus already revolting against fascism, for he is critical of what "has formed itself in the vast movements of crowds regulated by a ceremony introducing symbols to subjugate them."[45] Since the specter of fascist crowds haunts communal movements, I will return to these ceremonies.

More avowed, but also less known, is Acéphale's official and more scholarly counterpart, Le Collège de sociologie (1937–39), which Bataille cofounded with Roger Caillois and Michel Leiris to account for the surge of irrational, contagious, and sacred forces that were taking possession of the European body politic in the 1930s. Participants and attendees included figures like Alexandre Kojève, Denis de Rougement, Jean Wahl, and Walter Benjamin, among others, who, starting in 1937, assembled to give or listen to lectures on topics as diverse as animal societies and human societies, tragedy and literature, sacrifice and festivals, love and shamanism, power and sexuality, fascist communities and revolutionary communities, among other subjects.

Given the figures involved, the topics addressed, and the influence of Hegel and Nietzsche, Mauss and Durkheim, one can only imagine that, had he been born a decade earlier, Girard's name would have appeared among the participants of the Collège. In many ways, mimetic theory is a continuation of an epistemic principle inscribed in their founding "Declaration": trying to go beyond the confines of "literature" and "politics," they realized that "science"—by which they meant social science, primarily anthropology—"confined itself too much to the analysis of structures in so-called primitive societies, leaving aside modern societies."[46] "Sacred sociology," not unlike mimetic theory, was a collective, transdisciplinary effort to study the "social existence in all of its manifestations where the active presence of the sacred is felt" as a "pharmakon" that functioned as both "poison and cure"[47]—a pharmaceutical lesson central to Girard's theory of violence as well.

And yet, while Denis Hollier made the lectures of the Collège available in 1979 and an English translation has been in print since 1988,[48] the role of the Collège as an elective community that contributed to giving birth to contemporary theoretical accounts of community along lines that resonate with mimetic theory has not yet received the attention it deserves. This is surprising, for it is at the Collège that Bataille, along with Caillois, first developed a "sacred sociology" to account for the experience of a mimetic community on the basis of what he called "science of heterology."[49]

While still partially in line with a "Durkheimian perspective,"[50] Bataille's general interest was less in giving a homogeneous account of community understood as a social fact, and more in grounding the value of the sacred in general, and community in particular in what he calls "ontological" considerations "on the nature of society."[51] Heterology, as the name suggests, drew on impressively heterogeneous disciplinary discourses (or *logoi*), such as ontology, phenomenology, anthropology, sociology, psychology, and biology. And yet, as Denis Hollier makes clear, these "apprentice sociologists disguised in medicine men"[52] fin-de-siècle, organicist views of society promoted. Rather, it is based on what he calls a "communal movement" (*mouvement communiel*), a phrase that blends the religious register of communion with the social one of community.[55] Either way, this movement is affective in origins, generates violent fluxes of attraction and repulsion that are heterogeneous in nature, and rests on an ontology of becoming rather than of being.

For Bataille, then, community finds in sacred experiences that generate ecstatic horror the affective source of a contradictory double movement that both unites and divides the social body: death, sacrifice, tragedy are but the most prominent sacred experiences that constitute the palpitating heart or "central core" (*noyau central*) of community.[56] We reach here the core of Bataille's theory of the sacred, and what we find is something strikingly similar to, yet not entirely isomorphous with, Girard's account of sacrifice as the founding mechanism at the origins of culture.

Both Bataille and Girard, in fact, fundamentally agree that the sacred is rooted in sacrifice and violence, and that this violence spreads contagiously from self to others, generating a dissolution, or crisis, of difference. And yet, it is also important to note that rather than positing a cathartic theory of sacrifice whose purpose is to "restore harmony to the community, to reinforce the social fabric,"[57] Bataille stresses the discordant, oscillating movement that swings the community toward/away from the sacrificial center, both uniting the members and threatening to dissociate them. Bataille is here already investigating the emergence of polarized (heterogeneous) forces that are ontological in nature, generate what later theorists will call *partage*, and go to the metaphysical foundations of what he calls communal movements. This movement is a mimetic movement in the sense that it generates a double movement. As Bataille puts it, the "attraction and repulsion" that turns a part of the subject's "proper being to the profit of a communal being" is particularly visible in what he calls, echoing Nietzsche, the "herd."[58] As animals tend to assemble in a unique movement to form a herd, so members of a human herd are subjected to the same mimetic force of attraction, which is particularly strong in the presence of a master. And yet, at the same time, Bataille also specifies that a counter-movement of repulsion emerges as a subject that is unwittingly pulled into this opens the subject to the other, generating what Blanchot calls "the rapport with the other that is community itself"?[62]

Conjuring the figure of Dionysus in order to account for irrational, communal experiences that entail eroticism, sacrifice, death, but also drunkenness, festivities, and laughter, which are eminently contagious insofar as they turn an individual pathos into a shared pathos, Bataille posits what he calls "contagion" or "sympathy" at the basis of this rapport. Hence, still at the Collège, he specifies that the heterogeneous movements at the center of community are predicated on what he calls "the well-known principle of contagion, or if you want, shared feeling, sympathy."[63]

The principle of contagion, or sympathy, generates community. How? Through communication of an affect (*pathos*) whose defining characteristic is to be *shared* (*sym-pathos*); and it is on this principle of sharing (*partage*), which connects, like an undercurrent, self and other(s), that contagious communal movements flow. Nancy is thus again faithful to Bataille as he stresses that "the unleashing of passion" central to communal experiences "is of the order of what Bataille himself often designated as '*contagion*,'" which, he specifies, is "another name for 'communication,'" and thus for community as well.[64]

Contagion, communication, community. What is the principle that brings these discontinuous concepts together? This is the moment to recall the work Nancy shared with his philosophical alter ego and key figure in the genealogical connection between poststructuralism and mimetic theory, Philippe Lacoue-Labarthe. In their work in common, contagion is also another name for what the so-called Lacoue-Nancy duo repeatedly call—in a clear allusion to Girard—"imitation," "mimetism," or "mimesis." In an essay titled "The Nazi Myth," which I will discuss in more detail in the next chapter, the two philosophers understand mimesis not as Apollonian representation based on a unitary, static, and homogeneous form. Rather, they understand it as a contagious, affective, and heterogeneous "energy capable of effecting . . . identification" or "participation," "of which the best example is the Dionysian experience, as described by Nietzsche."[65]

In the wake of influential poststructuralist readings of Bataille, the powers of Dionysian mimesis and its conceptual and affective avatars (identification, contagion, fusion, etc.) have been restricted in favor of a general economy of linguistic "difference,"[66] a tendency that continues up to the present. And yet, we are now in a position to establish a genealogical link between theories of community and mimetic theory. Singularities, for Bataille, are shared on the basis of a mimetic principle that opens up the subject to the other, generating a contagious flow of energy that is easily shared, dissolves individual boundaries, and allows signifying differences to progressively slide into a torrent of affective sameness.

As a precursor of mimetic theory, or rather, a mimetic theorist himself, Bataille was fully aware that a contagious principle was at the heart of the experience of community. Thus, later in his career, in *Inner Experience*, speaking under the Nietzschean mask of "Dionysos philosophos," he convokes the experience of "contagion and mime" in order to define communal movements of "fusion," "ecstasy," "trance," or "general dramatization" (*dramatisation générale*), in which, he unequivocally says, "a man is a mirror of another man."[67]

To be sure, there are different ways in which humans mirror one another. For Bataille, this mirroring principle does not set up a unitary, stabilizing image that is reflected and seen from a (Apollonian) distance. Rather, what Bataille focuses on are mirroring, nonverbal, bodily (Dionysian) communications at play in communal experiences (laughter, tears, sacrifice, eroticism, love) that transgress the boundaries of individuation.[68] This is what Girard recognizes as he writes that "the notion of *dépense* in Bataille is clearly orgiastic and dionysiac, and therefore very violent."[69] Bataille not only accepted this connection; he also tied this violence to mimesis. As he repeatedly puts it, in the experience of mimetic communication the distinction between subject and object, self and other, one wave and another wave, no longer holds and what remains is the "movement," "flux," "contagion," "frenzy," or "fusion" that dissolves the ego in torrents that pave the way for what Bataille calls "the coming of a phantom" (*venue du fantôme*) or "whatever being" (*l'être quelconque*).[70]

A phantom has, indeed, been haunting theories of community: the phantom of mimesis. Hence Bataille writes, for instance, that in communal experiences "the subject and the object are dissolved, there is a passage, communication, but not from one to the other; the one and the other have lost their distinct existence." Or, in a more confessional, mimetic mood: "I cannot establish a difference between myself and those with whom I desire to communicate."[71] The singular ego, for Bataille, is not sealed off from others outside but emerges in a relation of mimetic communication with a plurality of others who are already inside.

Mimesis not as a simple mirror of the ego to be seen from a *distance* (or mimetic representation) then; but, rather, mimesis as a mirroring relation between humans that is felt in formless movements of communal ecstasy or *pathos* (mimetic dramatization): this *is* the affective and infective force that, for Bataille, sets the flux and reflux of communal movements in motion, dissolving the boundaries of the ego into a formless torrent of contagious communication that threatens to pull a different being into a movement of becoming similar—if not the same. The *ek-static* experience of mimesis *is* the torrential flow that brings the mimetic community into being, generating ontological continuities at the heart of Being.

I am using Nancy's image here, but genealogical lenses reveal that this torrent is already shared. The origins stem from a thinker who was not unfamiliar with the loneliness of Alpine peaks where such streams initially form and which Bataille was, in turn, quick to rechannel—allowing these torrential currents to reach, subterraneously, into the present. Bataille's affective and conceptual sources of community, in fact, do not stem from a sense of "originality," but from a mimetic experience he shares, first and foremost, with Nietzsche. Thus, he says: "The desire to communicate is born in me out of a feeling of community binding me to Nietzsche, and not out of an isolated originality."[72] Bataille is here contributing to Girard's exposure of the romantic *mensonge* of originality; and he does so on the shoulders of a figure who occupies a key place in mimetic theory.

Unsurprisingly, then, a genealogy of the mimetic community brings us back to a Nietzschean form of Dionysian communication. Here is the passage that provides Bataille and, at one additional remove, Nancy, with the torrential image at the heart of community. It appears in one of those untimely questions addressed to the future: "But where do those waves of everything that is great and sublime in man finally flow? Is there not an ocean for these torrents?" asks Nietzsche in a fragment of *Will to Power*, which Bataille re-presents (presents again) in *Inner Experience*.[73] And Bataille, who, "in the vast flux of things," considers himself "only a stopping point favorable to a resurgence,"[74] channels these currents for others to follow, as he immediately echoes:

> In experience, existence is no longer limited. A
> man cannot distinguish himself from others here
> in any way: in him what is torrential [*torrentiel*]
> in others is lost. Such a simple commandment: 'be
> that ocean,' linked to the extremity, makes man at
> once a multitude and a desert. It is an expression
> that summarizes and makes precise a sense of
> community. I know how to respond to Nietzsche's
> desire speaking of a community having no object
> but experience (but designating that community I
> speak of a desert).[75]

The desert of community, most theorists agree, is now growing. But so is what Nancy, echoing Bataille, echoing Nietzsche, calls the "torrent" constitutive of communal experiences.

From Nietzsche to Bataille, Blanchot to Nancy, and beyond, a powerful undercurrent in critical thought has repeatedly stressed the revolutionary side of torrential experiences that open up multiple possibilities of being in common—and this undercurrent is carrying us still. Thus, while Nancy prefers to speak of "revolt" (rather than revolution), he stresses the nondiscursive, communal force that generates what he calls a "common growl," as he writes: "Revolt does not discourse, it growls" (*gronde*). And he asks: "What does 'growl' mean?" Answer: "It means . . . becoming indignant, protest, become enraged together. One tends to grumble alone, but people growl in common."[76]

Why? Because growling is a mimetic experience. Indeed, a genealogical tradition confirms that nonverbal, contagious, and thus mimetic torrents can assemble people to growl in common, generating fluxes of revolt that revitalize phantoms of lost communities. This is a vital, affirmative side of communal formation that does not entail fusion in a mimetic pathos but allows for some pluralist distance to emerge. Mimesis can thus play a role in what Judith Butler calls a "performative theory of assembly" and William Connolly calls a "pluralist assemblage" internal to a "politics of swarming."[77]

And yet, at the same time, and without contradiction, as revolts generate common growls, the very same mimetic tradition has always cautioned us against the unpredictable turns such currents can already take. This risk is accentuated when the different modalities of being in common give way to the frenzied experience of mimetic sameness. That is, what Girard, thinking of the "orgiastic" and "violent" side of the dionysiac, calls "crisis of differences," characteristic of a "community literally undifferentiated [*dédifférenciée*], deprived of all that differs."[78]

We have reached a crossroads in our genealogy of community in which different currents of thought meet and generate spiraling effects that make us wonder: is community the potential locus of a mimetic revolt (Nancy)? Can a communal crisis be resolved via a violent sacrificial mechanism with cathartic effects that bring the community together (Girard)? Or can communal movements of attraction and repulsion both potentially oppose but also exacerbate a crisis that is constitutive of the mimetic community (Bataille)? All three options are open in theory, and we should not advocate between these possibilities, given the destabilizing properties of mimesis. Yet, from a genealogical perspective attentive to the emergence of communities in the 1920s and 1930s, it is necessary to remember that the experience of revolt against fascism can quickly capitulate to the same mimetic forces it sets out to oppose—and vice versa.

In the experience of phantoms of community, Bataille cautions us, "a man cannot distinguish himself from others" and "the torrent is lost," which does not mean that currents of mimetic contagion stop operating—on a massive and quite common scale. In this untimely reminder of the revolting turns phantom communities can take as differential currents pour into an ocean of sameness lies, perhaps, Bataille's mimetic originality.

The Phantom of Community

Before articulating his theory of community on the basis of an inner experience that is currently being recuperated on the theoretical scene, Bataille set out to diagnose the heterogeneous forces responsible for the emergence of outbreaks of mimetic contagion at the heart of the political scene. A genealogical step further back from Bataille's celebration of acephalic communities in the late 1930s to his critique of monocephalic leaders that have the power to generate an attraction to abject forms of ecstatic communion in the early 1930s, will allow us to leap ahead and bring his diagnostic of communal movements back to our present political concerns with (new) fascism.

In particular, Bataille supplements accounts of elective communities predicated on sharing and difference with a penetrating diagnostic of monocephalic communities in which "the agitations of phantoms" generate fusion and sameness.[79] He also balances Girard's hypothesis that violence serves a cathartic social function that brings the community together in light of a notion of sovereign communication that cannot be put to productive social use. "Fascism," he reminds us, "means reunion, concentration" (from Italian, *fascio*, bundle or sheaf),[80] and this concentration of a bundle (*fascio*) in a single leader (or head) can trigger violent movements of attraction and repulsion that lead to a squandering communal resolution in the body politic (or communal body). And once again, the inner/outer experience of *mimesis* is the fulcrum that turns communal revolts against figures of authority into revolting capitulations to phantasmal figures of authority.

In many ways, Bataille's investigations of the heterogeneous forces at the heart of "communal movements" at the Collège emerge as a revolt against the rise of fascist movements based on an organic conception of *Gemeinschaft* he radically opposes. Blanchot is thus right to stress that as the horrors of the fascist *Volk* became palpable in the late 1930s, Bataille was increasingly "repelled" by a "fusion" of individuals in a communal torrent of "collective effervescence" (*cela lui répugne profondément*).[81] Along similar lines, Nancy stresses Bataille's "resistance to fusion," but he also goes further as he sets up a conceptual distance between

Bataille's account of "community" on the one hand, and what he calls "common being," of which the fascist fusion is the most prominent manifestation, on the other.[82]

Indeed, Bataille's militant efforts in founding activist journals like *Contre-attaque*, where he countered the fascist appropriations of Nietzsche's thought, for instance, was precisely motivated by his opposition to what he called "fascist misery" in which "vulgar force" induces "endless slavery."[83] As he specifies, "modern dictators were reduced to finding their force by identifying themselves with all the impulses Nietzsche despised in the masses."[84] Similarly, his communal efforts at the Collège to study the unconscious power of the sacred as "the specific fact of society's communal movement"[85] is, as he and his collaborators clearly stated in their opening "Declaration" in 1937, "radically opposed to fascist aggression." Bataille's political resistance from the mid-1930s onward is real, should be taken literally, and offers an early example of how a theory of mimesis can be put to use to resist fascist contagion.

And yet, Bataille's defense of Nietzsche contra the fascist slavery might actually be, at least in part, a mirroring self-defense. On a closer genealogical look, in fact, Bataille's distinction between the elective community and the fascist community, sharing and fusion in the *early* 1930s, is not always as clear-cut as it appears to be, insofar as both communal movements are predicated on heterogeneous (i.e., sovereign) forms of communication that generate *ek-stasis*. This is the Dionysian side of mimesis, which, as Girard recognized, generates a "decadent" aesthetic pull on the general economy of Bataille's thought in general, and his communal thought in particular—what Girard calls "the only spice capable of stimulating the jaded appetite of modern man."[86]

Girard is not alone in this evaluation. After setting up a conceptual polarity between the ecstasy of fascism and the sharing of community, Nancy writes, in a move that earned him Blanchot's "reproach," that "for Bataille the pole of ecstasy remained linked to the fascist orgy," and specifies that "Bataille himself remained suspended, so to speak, between the two poles of ecstasy and community."[87] Nancy is right to notice that Bataille's position, like many others, remained, for a short period, "suspended" in an in-between oscillation of attraction to *ek-stasis* and repulsion from the fusion it entails.[88] As we have seen, this subjective oscillation mirrors the object of study, in the sense that this syncopated double movement is the beating heart of communal experiences as Bataille understands them.

My mimetic supplement—or rather echo—concerns a related but more fundamental level. Nancy's theoretical opposition between the "two poles" assumes that a boundary between fascist ecstasy and communal sharing exists, in which, as he says, "each [pole] limits the other."[89] For Bataille, however, this conceptual boundary is not impermeable to mimetic affects, but permeable and porous at best. The specificity of the general movement of Bataille's communal thought is, in fact, that it transgresses precisely such "limits."

In this transgression of limits, and the accursed Dionysian matters it reveals, the relevance of Bataille's diagnostic of (new) fascist forms of sovereign communication becomes fully apparent.

Bataille was not spellbound by linguistic binary oppositions that would provide an elementary structure at the foundations of society. Given his influence on poststructuralist philosophers like Jacques Derrida, it is no wonder that he is also close to Girard in stressing that mimetic movements function both as "an evil [*mal*] and as a remedy [*remède*]."[90] Or, to put it in our Nietzschean language, these movements trigger both a pathology and a patho-*logy*. The pathology in Bataille's mimetic thought leads him to posit the patho-*logical* possibility that communal weapons against fascism can actually backfire. As Bataille poignantly asks: "How can one know whether a movement that initially designates itself as anti-fascist, will not turn, more or less rapidly, towards fascism?"[91] This is a danger worth considering in light of the radical political indeterminacy of mimetic movements. Both at the collective level (sacred/fascist communities) and intersubjective level (communities of friends/lovers), the ecstasy of fusion, for Bataille, is always internal to the forms of mimetic sharing that are already constitutive of community—and therein lies precisely their dangerous fascination.

While attempting to keep these conceptual polarities apart in theory, Nancy simultaneously acknowledges that, in affective practice, they also "give rise to one another"[92]— and it is this second claim that, in my view, is closest to the movement of Bataille's communal thought. It would be useless to deny it: the experience of community is, indeed, haunted by the phantom of fascism and the "grotesque or abject resurgence of an obsession with communion" it entailed.[93] Later, speaking in the aftermath of the 9/11 attacks, Nancy will be more explicit as he notices the potentially dangerous confusions between the theoretical interest in community and "the revival of communitarian trends that could be fascistic."[94] Starting from post–World War II political preoccupations, Girard will postulate that this revival signals "a new stage in the escalation to extremes."[95] Since the dawn of the twenty-first century, the danger has only been escalating.

These are important preoccupations that have not received the attention they deserve in contemporary discourses on community. And yet, they reveal the double movement we have seen at the heart of the mimetic community from the beginning, which is now operative in (new) fascist movements as well. Just as the sacred has both a "right" (pure) side that elicits attraction and a "left" (impure) side that elicits repulsion,[96] so, in a mirroring inversion, politics can lead to revolts against fascism on the radical left and revolting capitulations to fascism on the extreme right. The indeterminacy of the sacred, in other words, mirrors the indeterminacy of the political. Unsurprisingly so since they both rest on mimetic principles.

Consequently, a critical account (*logos*) in the name of an affect (*pathos*) that is already shared (*sym-pathos*) always runs the risk of being caught in a torrent of fascination for abject communal pathologies. The terms Nancy uses to designate the fascist community ("abject," "common," "fusion," etc.) are, in fact, not simply terms of denigration. They are Bataille's diagnostic *concepts* convoked to dissect the *affective* forces of attraction and repulsion internal to what he calls "the psychological structure" that gives "unity to fascism."[97]

How is fascist unity achieved? On the basis of what Bataille already calls, in his "Essai de définition du fascisme," an "irrational attraction" in which each partisan "identifies with this leader."[98] And in a passage that anticipates Nancy and provides an important supplement to our genealogy of community, Bataille specifies that this "attracting action" entails a "*partage*," by which he means a paradoxical force that "divides what it attracts" (*sépare ce qu'elle attire*), generating in the process a "turbulent social scum" (*turbulent lie sociale*).[99] Bataille's insights into the pathological forces of *partage* responsible for the will to power of fascist leaders are, more than ever, in need of critical inquiries, especially in a period in which elective communities are withdrawing into the desert, while new torrents of fascist revolts are advancing on different fronts and are massively shared with an increasing speed and power of contagion.

In the wake of the rise of new fascist movements, the danger of contagion is once again taken seriously by political theorists. For instance, in *Aspirational Fascism*, William Connolly recently pointed out the urgency of diagnosing what he calls the "rhetoric of fascism," an infective rhetoric contagious affects the totalitarian leader "communicates" to the crowd,[101] which, as we know, generates ecstatic, fusional, and contagious identifications, Bataille zeroed in on the spiraling double movement at play in the rise of fascist communities. He was thus quick to realize that the experience of mimesis goes beyond good and evil insofar as it can turn from engaged *revolt* against authority into *revolting* subordinations to authority. And as a spiraling circulation of mimetic communication between the sovereign leader and the polarized crowd is set in motion, Bataille specifies that "the contagious affect" spreads "from house to house, suburb to suburb, suddenly turn[ing] a hesitant man into one who is no longer himself [*hors de soi*]"—that is, *ek-static.*[102]

The heterogeneous double movements Bataille posits at the heart of *acephalic communities* had already appeared, in their debased, abject form, as subjects are subjected to phantasmal leaders that turn the body politic into a *monocephalic crowd*. Bataille's starting point was not original, but emerged from previous mimetic theories. He drew from emerging human sciences such as anthropology, psychoanalysis, and especially crowd psychology. Thus, in an early essay titled

"The Psychological Structure of Fascism" (1932/33), Bataille focused on the mimetic rhetoric, affective mimicry, and infective gesticulations employed by fascist leaders to trigger communal movements of attraction and repulsion that, in turn, generate spiraling torrents of mimetic identification.

We swing from a body without a head to a body politic with a head, from the concept of "community" (*communauté*) back to the one of "crowd" (*foule, masse*). Still, the mimetic experience remains uncannily similar: it designates a heterogeneous double movement that always runs the risk of introducing continuity at the heart of discontinuity, thereby turning individual difference into collective sameness, a shared community into a phantom community.

Now, if the crowd gives body to these structural movements, crowd psychology was the social science that emerged in fin-de-siècle Europe to reflect on this disconcerting mimetic phenomenon. Furthering pioneering explorations by Sigmund Freud, and before him, Gustave Le Bon and Gabriel Tarde, whose work we discussed in the previous chapter, Bataille zoomed in specifically on the visceral/mimetic register employed by "fascist leaders" (*meneurs*

Indeed, when laws are broken, and the mimetic community remains under a spell of phantom leaders who are "totally other," fascist transgressions have already taken place. But they also stand a chance of being identified. Hence the need to look back to phantoms of the past to cast light on their new appearances in the present.

Fascist leaders, old and new, are "heterogeneous" in the specific Bataillean sense that, in theory, they do not subscribe to the sphere of productive, democratic, and rational principles (i.e., the homogeneous). Instead, they unleash an expenditure of useless, irrational, violent, and sexually charged pathos that in traditional societies was re-produced and squandered in ritual arenas anthropology grouped under the rubric of the "sacred," but now circulates in "civilized" political arenas as well (i.e., the heterogeneous).[104]

This mimetic circulation of irrational, Dionysian forces is what Bataille will later call our "accursed share" (*part maudite*). We might have moved away from religious rituals, yet the ambivalent force of the sacred, and the transgression of taboos it generates, continues to be visibly shared on political stages. Thus, Bataille adds that fascism turns a "homogeneous" society into a "heterogeneous" society in which leaders who are totally other trigger "affective reactions" (*réactions affectives*) that "are not only difficult to study, but whose existence has not yet been the object of a positive definition."[105]

One hundred years later, and the horrors of the twentieth century behind us, we have not come much further in the study of these mimetic movements—perhaps because they call for a type of diagnostic investigation predicated not only on external observations from a distance but also on the phenomenological engagement with the inner pathos of "lived states" (*états vécus*).[106] Now, Bataille relied precisely on this double interior/exterior patho-logical perspective as he articulated a diagnostic of fascist pathologies, which has largely gone unnoticed so far—perhaps because we lacked precisely such infective experiences.

In the wake of the recent resurgence of new leaders who reload mimetic mechanisms commonly employed by fascist leaders, such experiences are no longer lacking. Bataille's diagnostic should now strike a cord and is worth quoting in full, if only because it casts light on the most disconcerting powers of attraction characteristic of (new) fascist leaders:

> Considered not with regard to its external action but with regard to its source, the *force* of a leader [*meneur*] is analogous to that exerted in hypnosis. The affective flux that unites him with his followers [*partisans*]—which takes the form of a moral identification of the latter with the one they follow (and reciprocally)—is a function of the common consciousness of increasingly *violent* and *excessive* [*démesurés*] energies and powers that accumulate in the person of the leader and, through him, become widely available. But this concentration in a single person intervenes as an element that sets the fascist formation apart within the *heterogeneous* realm: by the very fact that the affective effervescence [*effervescence affective*] leads to unity, it constitutes, as *authority*, an agency directed *against* men; this agency is an existence for itself before being useful; an existence for itself distinct

from that of a formless uprising where for itself signifies 'for the men in revolt.' This monarchy, this absence of all democracy, of all fraternity in the exercise of power—forms that do not exist only in Italy or Germany—indicates that the immediate natural needs of men must be renounced, under constraint, in favor of a transcendent principle that cannot be the object of an exact explanation.

In a quite different sense, the lowest strata of society can equally be described as heterogeneous, those who generally provoke repulsion and can in no case be assimilated by the whole of mankind.[107]

The principle might be elusive and escape exact homogeneous explanations; yet Bataille offers a searching diagnostic of the spiral of mimetic communication that leads from the sharing at play in "communal movements" to the fusion of a "common consciousness" constitutive of the (new) fascist crowd nonetheless.

The spiraling movement of this passage contains, in

embryo, the general psychic economy of the structure of fascism, as Bataille understands it, and can be disentangled in the following diagnostic lessons that inform new fascism as well and that I summarize in guise of conclusion.

Five Lessons on (New) Fascist Transgression

First, Bataille specifies that fascist leaders do not rely on reason or consciousness but on "hypnosis" and "identification" to steer the masses during "democratic" elections. That is, fascist leaders trigger eminently contagious affects that, as Nietzsche also noted, operate on the physio-psychological level; are registered below the threshold of consciousness; generate reflex, hypnotic actions and reactions; and are, in this specific sense, both *mimetic* and *unconscious*.

This mimetic unconscious is not mediated by a metapsychology that divides identification from desire: it's rather a question of the masses unconsciously mirroring the heterogeneous *pathos* of the leader. Hence Bataille specifies that "the *unconscious* must be considered as one of the aspects of the *heterogeneous*."[108] Put in our language, (new) fascist leaders do not operate on the register of rational consciousness; rather, they rely on heterogeneous matters that are traditionally linked to the sacred (sacrifice, violence, abject matters, sexual transgressions, etc.) to trigger the mimetic unconscious of a crowd already suggestible to hypnotic influences.

Second, such leaders direct violence against "foreign societies" (*sociétés étrangères*) and oppressed social groups,[109] most notably the "lowest strata" of the population, leading them, by hypnotic means that take possession of their rational ego, to actively promote—somnambulist-like—the very leaders qua phantoms that dispossess them. One year later, in "The Notion of Expenditure," Bataille addresses the interplay of racial and class discrimination in the United States in diagnostic terms that still speak to the contemporary political crisis. As he puts it, "In particular in the United States, the primary process [of expenditure] takes place at the expense of only a relatively small portion of the population: to a certain extent, the working class itself has been led to participate in it (above all, when this was facilitated by the preliminary existence of a class held to be abject by common accord, as in the case of the blacks)."[110]

Bataille is writing in the 1930s, but despite the progress generated by civil rights movements in the 1960s, his diagnostic still holds for the 2010s. In fact, the degree of working-class participation in the process of U.S. capitalist expenditure (aka the American Dream), which is the privilege of an increasingly smaller portion of the population, has been significantly reduced over the past decades; working-class subjects find themselves increasingly linked to abject social conditions they share with other disenfranchised segments of the population, most notably racial minorities. And yet, this shared economic disenfranchisement between white working-class, African American, and other ethnic minorities who are kept at the margins of the capitalist dream does not generate a *partage* based on *sym-pathos*. On the contrary, it can trigger a violent pathological need on the side of the white working class to escalate a racist distance instead.

The mimetic pathology is not deprived of an affective logic that sets in motion a pathos of distance based on attraction and repulsion. In fact, the need for working-class distance from racial minorities is felt more intensely as unions that would allow for shared bonds of sympathy based on a shared economic oppression to cut across the racial divide are dismantled. In the process, economic differences and social distinctions between these minorities decrease, while the distance from the American Dream increases, so as to render it attainable for few and unattainable for most.

As the dream reveals itself to have been a fictional image far removed from reality (some would say a lie), working-class resentment escalates in real life. It does so due to the spiraling interplay between real social oppression and heterogeneous fascist rhetoric. Thus, the fascist leader (or head) injects a violent pathos into already angry crowds (or social body), channeling heterogeneous directed against the racial minorities who share a common neoliberal oppression—doubled by a stubborn structural racism that never made the dream really attainable for the latter in the first place. This mimetic patho(-)logy can then be effectively exploited by new fascist leaders who rely on heterogeneous forces to direct white working-class frustration, ressentiment, fear, and anger against racial, but also sexual and religious minorities, immigrants, and other marginalized scapegoats, who are held abject by a common accord, a racist-sexist-religious-hypernationalist-white accord that still manages to tie—via an imaginary and increasingly phantasmal dream of greatness—white elites to the working-class subjects they so effectively exploit.

Third, this mimetic identification between leader and crowds is "reciprocal" and cuts both ways. In the process it generates a spiraling feedback loop with cumulative polarizing effects that, Bataille later specifies, "generates a movement of concentration of power" in fascist heads.[111] If we break down the psychic economy of this spiraling movement, we see (and feel) that the hypnotized crowd (or social body) sets up a narcissistic mirror to the leader (or head) who, in turn, identifies with the crowd's mirroring impulses and, therefore, feels—by way of mimetic contagion—himself increasingly empowered by these violent and excessive forces he catalyzed.

Head and body are now part of what Bataille calls "common consciousness" that has become "widely available" in the body politic. The recent proliferation of new media redoubles the effect. It amplifies this common consciousness by generating spiraling loops that go from the crowd who is part of a physical body to the virtual publics who make this consciousness widely available in the proliferating net of digital communities as well, to the leader himself who is (mis)informed by these media—in an endless spiraling regress that allows for foreign cyber-interferences currently under investigation, which lead the body politic away from the light of consciousness toward the darkness of the mimetic unconscious.

Fourth, this "accursed share," as Bataille will later call it, is composed of irrational affective forces that are usually "excluded" by "homogeneous" rational capitalist societies, but continue, in covert and less covert ways, to be shared, especially during those sacred rituals we profanely call elections. They include the sphere of the "unconscious," "violence," "madness," "sexuality," "bodily parts," including "words or acts having a suggestive erotic value" (*valeur érotique suggestive*),[112] among other heterogeneous taboo experiences that can be transgressed during (new) fascist revolts.

Bataille is touching on a delicate point that is often neglected in scholarly debates on fascism but is now visibly center stage in (new) fascism. As a former owner of Miss Universe pageants, Trump's political prestige cannot be disentangled from his type of patriarchal, sexualized, and phallocentric objectification of women that still casts a sexist spell on the contemporary imagination. This tendency has been aggravated by all kinds of heterogeneous sexual matters that have since emerged as constitutive of Trump's political persona: from his misogynist affirmations (women bleeding), predatory sexual behavior (grabbing genitals), affairs with porn stars (Stormy Daniels), not to speak of the shadow of lurid videotapes that promise to reveal abject subject matters (pee tape) that are now, nolens volens, part of the collective imagination, this accursed share is, indeed, viscerally *repulsive*—and this repulsion has generated positive, empowering antifascist movements.

In particular, it has led to massive transnational protests such as the "Me Too" movement, which casts a much overdue limelight on sexual harassment and assault on women who are now encouraged to speak out contra abusive bosses or leaders, including phallocentric political leaders. This vital reaction shows that alternative communal counter-movements can and should indeed emerge as a reaction to patriarchal, sexist tendencies exacerbated by (new) fascist leaders. This exemplary movement should thus be imitated and amplified to defend other minorities (in terms of race, sexual orientation, class, nationality, religion, age, etc.) stretching to include the defense of the environment as well—the most recent and still underrepresented victim of (new) fascist governments.[113]

At the same time, and without contradiction, for a good part of Trump supporters, his sexual scandals might contribute, paradoxically, to his ongoing media success. If critics have had trouble accounting for this striking patho(-)logical paradox, Bataille's account of the *attractive* force of abject subject matters that generate repulsion provides a possible answer: (new) fascist politics capitalizes on a human fascination for an accursed share that cannot be restricted to so-called primitive cultures but is constitutive of "civilized" entertainment as well.

Violence and death, sex and porn: haven't these subject

matters been massively uploaded as transgressive spectacles in the sphere of the virtual? Bataille never tired of reminding us that no "civilized" nation is at bay from the spell of heterogeneous Dionysian forces. They are part of the accursed share that makes us human, all too human—and during transgressive political periods, potentially inhuman.

This is especially true if we consider that the mimetic movements of attraction and repulsion Bataille diagnosed with respect to fascist leaders and the heterogeneous sexual matters they are associated with are no longer restricted to the sphere of the sacred defined by taboos that can be occasionally transgressed in ritual contexts. Instead, they are proliferating in the profane sphere of adult entertainment that continuously simulates the experience of sexual transgression on digital screens. The manifestations of sexist behavior in political life must thus be framed in the context of a growing production and consumption of pornographic spectacles that are not only proliferating on the Internet, but, via the logic of hypermimesis, retroact on users transforming the sexual imaginary, practices, evaluations—including political evaluations—among a population increasingly exposed in the digital age but operate on the mimetic unconscious nonetheless and, above all, can be channeled in both fascist and anti-fascist directions.

The fifth and last Bataillean lesson, the bodily rhetoric channeled by (new) fascist leaders makes sure that in its affective charge there is "as much attraction as there is repulsion," so as to trigger a polarized double movement that has "the force of a shock" and swings the body politic in opposite directions: on the one hand, this mimetic pathos, which Bataille compares to electricity, threatens to tear it apart, producing a polarized heterogeneity in place of homogeneity that can fuel anti-fascist revolts; on the other hand, this discharge unleashes an homology within heterology in the sense that it generates a "unification" characterized by a "community of direction" (*communauté de direction*).[114]

On both sides, once caught in this common movement, Bataille specifies that the mimetic "subject has the possibility to displace the exciting value from one element to another, similar or neighboring element," along mirroring principles he compares to "conditioning Pavlovian reflexes."[115] Humans are proud of the conscious accomplishments of the spirit, and rightly so, for they can lead to progress, including social and political progress that can be put to anti-fascist patho-*logical* use. But we should not forget that we also have a body that responds to unconscious mimetic reflexes that can lead to regress and fascist pathologies. These Pavlovian reflexes have a conditioning power that is difficult to consciously control and do not set up a narcissistic image to a species that modestly defined itself as *Homo sapiens*. Still, this mirror reminds us of the imitative nature of what I prefer to call *Homo mimeticus*. In sum, the movement of the fascist community is heterogeneous in conceptual origins, but the mirroring principles that bring it into being are thoroughly mimetic in their affective force. Thus, the free subject becomes a docile subject; a shared community turns into a phantom community.

Such heterogeneous principles may not have been the "object of a precise explanation" at the beginning of the past century; and yet, the neurosciences have now confirmed the importance of mirroring reflexes in nonverbal forms of communication at the end of the twentieth century. What we said about affective contagion in general in the past chapter equally applies to the sexual and violent contagion diagnosed in this chapter: the discovery of "mirror neurons" in the 1990s lends empirical support to Bataille's untimely realization that subjects can respond unconsciously, that is, automatically, to (facial) gestures and expressions because the sight of such gestures triggers mirror neurons to fire, causing an unconscious reflex not only to reproduce the gestures, but also to feel, by way of what used to be called *sym-pathy*, the *pathos* of the other within the ego.

Hailed as a revolutionary scientific discovery central to "understanding,"[116] this nonlinguistic communication was well-known by pre-Freudian theorists of the mimetic unconscious. A mimetic tradition that goes from Nietzsche to Tarde, Wilde to Conrad, D. H. Lawrence to Bataille and many others, saw such reflexes at work not only for the purpose of "understanding the emotions of others" along nonverbal lines that facilitate "empathy,"[117] but its very opposite: namely, mass manipulation of affects that lead to violence instead—a mimetic violence that, as Girard never tired of repeating, is "contagious" and has the power to turn a "literally undifferentiated community" into what he calls, echoing a long tradition in crowd psychology, "a crowd [*foule*] that is at one with the obscure call that unifies it and that mobilizes it, that is that transforms it into a *mob*," which, he reminds us, comes from "*mobile*" and thus involves movement.[118]

This mobility of the crowd mirrors the mobility characteristic of (new) fascist leaders. Mimetic theorists have thus the responsibility to remind scientists that mimesis generates mirroring mechanisms that cut both ways: it is the source of logical insights into the working of mimetic pathos (or patho-logies) that can lead both to revolts contra fascism and, at the same time, to capitulations of contagious affects (or pathologies) that can lead to (new) fascist movements.

While inoperative communities on the side of revolts have received ample attention in recent years, in a balancing move mimetic theory reminds us that communities can become operative on the side of (new) fascist movements as well. In particular, Bataille's claim that a "negated crowd [*masse*], has ceased to be itself in order to become, affectively . . . part of the leader [*chef*] itself" accounts for the docile, irrational, affective, and thoroughly uncritical status of crowds that capitulate to the very leaders who violently negate them.[119] As he will later put it: "There is nothing in our world to parallel the capricious excitement of a crowd obeying impulses of violence with acute sensitivity and unamenable to reason."[120] While reason (or *logos*) has difficulties naming this mimetic impulse (or *pathos*), this does not mean that mimetic patho(-)logies are not already at play in mimetic communities.

To be sure, Bataille's untimely diagnostic that such leaders did "not exist only in Italy or Germany" is not only historically correct. It also captures, genealogically, the phantoms of community that continue to haunt the contemporary political scene. As we move from the old to the new fascism, the mass media used to trigger mass "movements" change— we move from newspapers to new media, the radio to the tweet—generating a regime of post-truth that will continue to require new types of mimetic diagnostics, for algorithms that track our digital habits, Internet preferences, and virtual behavior are already effectively programmed to exploit and radically amplify control of our psychic structure, rendering us more than mimetic, that is, hypermimetic.

To summarize and conclude: how does the rhetoric of (new) fascism work? By relying, first of all, on affective, hypnotic, embodied, and highly mimetic theatrical rhetoric staged on what Bataille calls, conjuring a classical scene, "the theatre where the political tragedy is played out."[121] Since classical antiquity, theorists have, in fact, known that the theater, and the actors that animate it, is not intended to promote useful, rational arguments (*logoi*) to inform political consciousness. On the contrary, it dispenses fluxes of mimetic affects (*pathoi*) that are at play in the sphere of unemployable entertainment, both comic and tragic. It is thus worth recalling that the concept of *mimesis* comes from the affective practice of the actor (*mimos*) who, from the origins of theory (from *theorein*, to see; linked to *theates*, spectator, from *thea*, a seeing but also a seat in the theater), relies on an eminently mimetic rhetoric to steer the unconscious of physical crowds—and, at an additional remove, of virtual publics as well.

Fascist rhetoric, I have argued, is mimetic rhetoric that triggers a shared communal pathos. Specifically, it entails repetition of national slogans; use of affective images;

mobilization of the skills of the actor (mimicry, facial expressions, grandiloquent tone, gesticulations, mixing of tragic and comic poses); stimulation of sad, tragic affects; designation of marginalized scapegoats on which such pathos is vented from a distance that prevents sympathy; solicitation of heterogeneous subject matters such as sex and violence, which trigger massive movements of attraction and repulsion—all of this accursed share channeled by a mass-mediatized culture in which an apprentice president turns politics into a play that is no longer sacred but profane, no longer unemployable but effectively employed. Hence new fascism even turns the unproductive sphere of the sacred to capitalist, usable, all too usable profit; the heterogeneous turns into the homogeneous. We can thus only join our voices to "protest" with Nancy "that existence is untenable if it doesn't open up spaces of sense."[122] And in a last mimetic growl that Nancy shares, among others, with Lacoue-Labarthe, and, at one remove, Girard as well, he adds that "this opening up of sense is impossible so long as what reigns instead of circulation is the pitiless circularity in which everything-amounts-to-the-same."[123]

famously called, in *Republic*, an "ancient quarrel between philosophy and poetry" whose effect was to split *muthos* and *logos* in rivalrous yet intimately related positions.[2] This binary was, in fact, far from clear-cut. *Muthos*, as Jean-Pierre Vernant reminds us, means "formulated speech," "belongs to the domain of *legein* . . . and does not originally stand in contrast to *logoi*."[3]

And yet, while they remained intertwined, Vernant also adds that by the fourth century, *muthos* was already in opposition to *logos* and contributed to shaping philosophy, in the sense that *logos* was defined by what *muthos* is not.[4] Classicists like Vernant, but also Eric Havelock, and before them Friedrich Nietzsche, compellingly argue that this turn from *muthos* to *logos* was pregnant with meaning: it entailed a shift from mythic characters that are manifold and changeable to ideal Forms that are unitary and immutable, from embodied fictional figures to disembodied intelligible Ideas, from the singularity of examples to the universality of types, but also from irrationality to rationality, orality to writing, *pathos* to *nous*, and, more generally, an ontology of becoming to one of Being. The mirroring inversion at play in this ancient antagonism suggests, then, that philosophy was born by pushing against a mythic womb.

In the process, what is still arguably the most influential Western critique of myth, namely, Plato's *Republic*, offered an evaluation that was at least double. Plato was, in fact, as much concerned with the content (*logos*) of mythic representations and the lies they promote as with the form (*lexis*) of dramatic spectacles and the pathos they mediate.

On the side of the message, the argument went, mythic texts like Homer's *Iliad* and Hesiod's *Theogony* do not represent the truth about the gods but promote fictional lies that, as Plato famously says in book 10, are at "three removes" from intelligible Forms (Plato, *Republic*, 597e). This is a picture of myth as an illusory copy, "shadow," or as he also says, "phantom" (*phantasma*) (601c) of reality that splits philosophy and myth apart, and is well-known on both sides of the divide.

On the other, perhaps less-known side, Plato argues in books 2 and 3 that mythic figures such as Achilles in *The Iliad* or Uranus in the *Theogony*, as they are not simply narrated from a diegetic distance, but rather dramatized on theatrical stages via actors or *mimes* who address in mimetic speeches imbued with pathos what Plato calls "the mob assembled in the theater" (604e)—these figures, he says, have a mysterious *formal* power to penetrate the psychic life of subjects and give form to their characters. This is no longer a picture, but rather a dramatization of myth as a formative model that has the power to generate not only copies or reproductions of reality, but also copies or productions of subjects.

Either way, the language of forms and models, shadows and phantoms that Plato convokes at the dawn of philosophy already identifies a double, or rather, protean concept that, to this day, continues to give power to myth: namely *mimēsis*, understood *both* as an aesthetic representation of reality *and* as an affective formation of subjects.

In very broad and admittedly partial strokes, this is, I believe, the double-protean concept that Philippe Lacoue-Labarthe never ceased to mediate as a Janus-faced philosopher-poet working at the juncture where *logos* and *muthos*, literature and philosophy, poetics and politics, face, confront, and above all reflect (on) each other.[5] If his work has remained somewhat in the shadows so far, following the conceptual protagonist he tirelessly chased throughout his polymorphous career (i.e., mimesis), this did not prevent history from shadowing forth political fictions and fictional phantoms that are currently confirming his penetrating diagnostic of the power of myth in real life.

Like Girard before him, Lacoue-Labarthe took seriously the Platonic connection between myth and mimesis, probably because he shared with Girard an appreciation of the power of literature in the Romantic period to cast light on the mimetic nature of human behavior. This proximity led to a differentiation between the two authors that, to this day, often splits them into competing camps: Girard, we are often told, is on the side of sameness and referentiality; Lacoue-Labarthe is on the side of difference and language. The former looks back to the beginning of culture to find the origins of mimesis; the latter looks ahead to the process of deferral of mimesis. One is critical of the view that mimesis entails (re)presentation; the other stresses the inevitability of re-*production*. One builds a mimetic system while the other is busy deconstructing mimesis. These differences are real and fundamental, and are constitutive of the two authors' agonal exchanges that punctuate some of their works.[6]

And yet, while these exchanges may be *agonal*, they remain *exchanges* nonetheless. I started by emphasizing Girard's relevance to account for the mimetic mechanisms that generate affective sameness at the heart of contemporary politics along lines resonant with crowd psychology (chapter 1). I now turn to Lacoue-Labarthe's explicit confrontation with the problematic of fascist and Nazi politics, which grows out of his joint reflections with Nancy on community (chapter 2). This perspective, as we shall see, cannot be reduced to linguistic traces confined to the "undecidability" of the sphere of "representation."[7] Rather, it addresses the problematic of affective contagion that remains central to reloading (new) fascist myths that now cast a shadow on the real, referential world.

Lacoue-Labarthe was particularly sensitive to the mimetic principles at play in mythic figures endowed with the double power to disfigure the truth, and perhaps more seriously, to impress, form, or in-*form* via a process he called "typography," impressionable and plastic subjects with the seal of authoritarian or fascist types. In the twentieth century, these types found their culmination in the horror of what Lacoue-Labarthe and Nancy called "The Nazi Myth," and as we are beginning to realize, far from being left behind by a grand mythic narrative of progress, these types are currently returning, phantom-like, to haunt the body politic in the twenty-first century as well.

I thus step back to "The Nazi Myth," a text that, as Jean-Luc Nancy recently says, was "often quoted" but "very little reworked" (*fort peu . . . retravaillé*),[8] in order to leap ahead, once again, to the resurgence of mythic figures in new fascist movements that are haunting the contemporary political scene. This perspective on myth follows naturally from the previous genealogy of crowds and communities. Lacoue-Labarthe and Nancy, in fact, both agreed with crowd psychology and mimetic theory that "one of the essential ingredients in fascism is *emotion*, collective, mass emotion";[9] they also agreed with Bataille and Girard that even when it is "interrupted," myth "is always 'popular'" and its power "cannot simply disappear."[10] Neither Girard nor Lacoue-Labarthe lived long enough to see their fears of the return of mimetic contagion amplified by new fascist leaders that effectively appeal to mass emotion on both sides of the Atlantic. Still, their mimetic theories provide, from different but related perspectives—Girard speaking from the side of the victim; Lacoue-Labarthe challenging the side of the victimizer—starting points to account for the renewed power of myth today.

Building on this heterogeneous tradition in mimetic theory, I pursue a diagnostic of the affective power of myth that can perhaps be summarized under the following, two-faced question: if, on one side, mythic figures or types generate what Plato calls in *Republic* "phantoms" (*phantasmata*) of reality (599a), that is, copies or shadows without ontological value that turn the world into a fiction, and on the other side, these figures bring into being what Nietzsche in *Daybreak*, writing with and against Plato, calls a "phantom of the ego" (*Phantom von Ego*),[11] that is, a copy or simulacrum of man without psychic substance that can reach massive proportions in real life—if this Janus-faced diagnostic of *mimesis* is true (and I see little evidence today that convinces me of the contrary), what, then, is the affective and formal mechanism that is currently reloading the power of myth today?

Having opened this book with a Girardian reading of mimetic mechanisms at play in mythic fictions from the point of view of the victim, I now invert perspective to look at it from the point of view of the mythic leader. I suggest that stepping back to Lacoue-Labarthe's and Nancy's untimely diagnostic of myth as a mimetic instrument that was massively deployed to disseminate the Nazi myth in the twentieth century gives us a timely starting point to unmask mythic principles that are now restaged by new fascist leaders in the twenty-first century. My wager is that reloading a genealogy of the power of myth starting from (*à partir de*) Lacoue-Labarthe provides us with a mirror to reflect *on* the mythic destinations where we could potentially, but not inevitably, end (*aller à finir*).

This genealogical connection between fascism in Europe and the phantom appearance of new forms of fascism in both Europe and the United States does not follow Lacoue-Labarthe's critique of myth à la lettre. In a 2002 interview with Peter Hallward, for instance, he explicitly refrained from stretching his critique of mimesis to include what Hallward calls "the national myth, or fantasy (the American dream)."[12] Lacoue-Labarthe even goes as far as making the following, admittedly provisional claim: "I may be wrong but it seems that up until now there have not been any *serious* problems regarding American identity"—a claim he nonetheless immediately qualifies by supplementing serious problems like "the unresolved problem of race," the "foreclosure of the original genocide, that of Native Americans," as well as the "mimetic" and "extremely conformist" dimension of U.S. identity politics.[13]

This supplement leads him to a second, more nuanced diagnostic: namely, that "if there is a problem of identity in the USA, the social organization is such that it gives rise to neurosis rather than psychosis."[14] The American national myth is thus pathologized. But even in the sphere of mental pathology, let alone political pathology, the binary dividing neurosis from psychosis is blurry at best. In any case, given Lacoue-Labarthe's recognition that in the wake of 9/11 "we are witnessing a revival of American nationalism," not to mention his repeated avowals that "he may be wrong" in his diagnostic,[15] his *political* evaluation does not foreclose alternative *genealogical* investigations of the power of myth—quite the contrary.

Reopening the dossier on myth *à partir de* Lacoue-Labarthe, then, cannot be restricted simply to applying his political diagnostic. Instead it involves reloading the general logic of mimesis to account for the return of mythic power in the contemporary period. This move is, in many ways, a natural one. After all, according to a paradoxical logic, or hyperbologic, that Lacoue-Labarthe rendered us sensitive to, precisely because postmodern nations are even farther removed than modern nations from their Western origins—*at three removes*, so to speak—they might paradoxically come closer to the dangers of fascist identifications with mythic figures who offer the promise of a unitary, self-enclosed, and stable national identity.

This hypothesis, at least, is one Lacoue-Labarthe and Nancy leave open at the end of "The Nazi Myth." In fact, they claim that the "mimetic will-to-identify . . . belongs profoundly to the mood or character of the West in general" (*la volonté mimétique d'identité . . . appartient profondément aux dispositions de l'Occident en général*)[16]—a point they subsequently confirm in the preface to the French edition, in which they claimed, thinking explicitly of "the most important 'democracy' in the world" (notice the quotation marks), that "democracy asks, or must ask the question of its 'figure' [*sa 'figure'*]."[17]

How such a mythic figure has the power to turn an old dream into a new nightmare is what we turn to find out.

Old Dream/New Nightmare

The mythic greatness of a nation tends to be the product of a dream. It is thus no wonder that it is with fictional dreams, rather than political realities, that new cases of authoritarian leaders are currently encouraging mythic identifications.

Drawing on the Puritan myth of the "chosen people" constitutive of "American Greatness," in the opening pages of *Great Again* (2015), Donald Trump conjures the image of the "shining city on a hill, which," he says, "other countries used to admire and try to be like."[18] This mythic image is constitutive of the American Dream, but the dream is not deprived of a mimetic logic that is at least double and has real effects: on one side, the reference to a mythic past is instrumental in promoting the view that the United States should again occupy the position of the model for all the world to copy in the future; on the other hand, the attempt of other countries to "be like" America in the past is used as a rhetorical strategy to direct U.S. voters' identification toward figures who dream to make America great again in the present. Either way, this double rhetorical move confirms that Lacoue-Labarthe's and Nancy's understanding of myth as an "instrument of identification" is currently being reloaded—and quite effectively so.

And yet, on the opposite political front, mirroring inversions of perspectives are already at play. Noam Chomsky, for instance, reminds us that this dream of greatness, while powerful, liberating, and inspiring in the past, has not been manifest in the present and casts a nightmarish shadow on the world's future. Thus, in *Requiem for the American Dream* (2017), Chomsky initially agrees *with* Trump that "the American Dream, like most dreams, has large elements of myth to it";[19] and yet, *contra* Trump, Chomsky sets out to remind us that while promising freedom for all in theory, in practice this exceptionalist, or better, nationalist myth was also founded on the extermination of a native population, racial segregation, working-class as well as immigrant exploitation, not to speak of the crusades, walls, nuclear threats, and anti-environmentalist politics it continues to generate on the basis of clear-cut mythic distinctions between good and evil, Christian and non-Christian, whites and nonwhites, truth and alternative truths, or, as we used to call them, lies.

It is in response to the loss of distinction between truth and lies in particular that genealogical reminders about the power of myth are especially important. As Hannah Arendt puts it in *The Origins of Totalitarianism* (1951), part of the "demoralizing fascination" of totalitarian leaders stems from "the possibility that gigantic lies and monstrous falsehoods can eventually be established as unquestioned facts."[20] Myth obviously plays a key role in the erasure of the difference between truth and falsehood. As George Mosse, a historian of the Holocaust, reminds us in *Nazi Culture* (1966): "Building myths and heroes was an integral part of the Nazi cultural drive" insofar as the "the flight from reason became a search for myth and heroes to believe in."[21] And he adds: "It is unfashionable to speak of the lessons of history, but perhaps there is a lesson for the present hidden among these documents of the past."[22]

The lesson may be unfashionable, but a growing number of scholars worried about the return of fascism are revisiting documents of the past in light of the present. More recently, Timothy Snyder in *On Tyranny* (2017) confirms this genealogical point as he cautions American readers in the wake of Trump's election that "Fascists rejected reason in the name of will, denying objective truth in favor of a glorious myth articulated by leaders who claimed to give voice to the people."[23] And considering the hypnotic power of myth mediated by new fascist spectacles, he also warns us of the following mimetic danger: "We stare at the spinning vortex of cyclical myth until we fall into a trance—and then we do something shocking at someone else's orders."[24]

On yet another front, in *Aspirational Fascism* (2017), William Connolly uncovers striking genealogical similarities between Hitler's and Trump's rhetorical styles designed to "distort democracy" and "draw a large segment of the population actively into the aggressive movement itself."[25] How? Among other strategies, by relegating opposition to the status of mythic lies, aka "fake news," while "mobilizing intensive mass energies to sustain itself as it weakens the media," thus rendering the "lines between consent and imposition blurry."[26]

These are just some recent examples. While not focusing specifically on mimesis, they resonate strongly with the study at hand. More are currently emerging, and others will certainly follow. They should nonetheless suffice to indicate that after a period of marginalization, myth and its relation to identification is clearly back to the forefront of the theoretical and political scene.

Theorists on different sides of the political spectrum agree on a series of related points: first, they posit myth at the center of the logic of new fascist dreams that operate on an immanent and embodied unconscious that has mimetic contagion as a *via regia*; second, they remind us of the ancient (Platonic) lesson that myth can be put to *both* totalitarian use (myth as a model to identify with) *and* critical use (myth as a lie to be unmasked); third, they caution us that the use of myth in emerging forms of authoritarian politics has the power to trigger massive identifications that generate a collective pathos on which new fascist movements prey; and fourth, they call for an urgent analysis of new fascist types—both in Europe and in the United States—that have the power to progressively erase the already thin line dividing truth from lies, fictions from politics—thus turning liberating dreams into a nightmarish reality.

There are thus sufficient reasons for bringing Lacoue-Labarthe back from the shadows; his double literary-philosophical sensibility opens up new perspectives that further the growing field of mimetic theory. As we are confronted with the return of new fascist phantoms on the political scene, his work persistently urges us to look back to the ancient use of myth in the past to avoid similar abuses in the future. Following this indication, a detour via a book Lacoue-Labarthe and Nancy consider central to what they call "the construction of the Nazi myth,"[27] namely, Alfred Rosenberg's *The Myth of the 20th Century* (1936), will allow us to reload the problematic of mythic types, figures, and dreams central to our diagnostic of fascist identification along genealogical lines that will eventually make us see and feel how the power of myth is currently being reloaded.

Genealogy of Myth and Types

Rosenberg referred to his book as "The Myth," indicating that it did not simply represent the power of Nordic myths, but actually attempted to reenact this power. First published in 1930, this book was certainly more bought than read and cannot be compared to its more popular double,

and Folk, economy becomes nomadic, life is uprooted," to his emphasis on a racist ideology that, he says, "still determines the ideas and actions of men, whether consciously or unconsciously," from his observation that "the sacrifice [of men during the Great War] was to the advantage of forces other than those for which the armies were ready to die," to his critique of common people's "subjugation under the dictates of international finance," to his realization that "chaos has today been elevated almost to a conscious program point,"[29] to other critiques that struck a chord among a suffering population, *The Myth of the 20th Century* reminds us that myth tends to be reloaded during periods of economic, political, national, and thus identity crisis—a crisis of identity that can always reemerge in other centuries and nations as well, including "democratic" nations.

For our purpose, however, it is Rosenberg's realization that the power of myth cannot be dissociated from the types that mediate it that is most directly relevant to our immediate theoretical and political preoccupations. As Rosenberg points out, in the wake of the World War I economic crisis, "nationalistic rebirth appears as so dangerous because from it a power, capable of forming Types, threatens to arise."[30] And in a section titled "Myth and Type," he specifies that the problematic of "myth" cannot be dissociated from the "types" it forms, for these types can give a unity to an identity the German people have lost and need to dream again. Hence, the task Nazism should set itself in order to recover this dream, he continues, is to "experience a Myth and to create a type"; and, he adds: "from out of this type we must build our state."[31]

Myth, type, and an experience out of which an ideal "image of the soul," and by extension, of the state, should serve as a "model" for other nations to copy.[32] To be sure, such formulations appear in the context of mythical fictions about Nordic, racial, and anti-Semitic ideals that lack any historical grounding and are characteristic of myth understood in its classical opposition to a rational *logos*—what Lacoue-Labarthe disparagingly calls in *La fiction du politique* an "authoritarian, voluntaristic logorrhea."[33]

And yet, at the same time, such types are also symptomatic of an underlying mythic logic that, as Lacoue-Labarthe and Nancy demonstrate, is constitutive of the ontological foundations of what they call the "logic of fascism,"[34] and, we should add, to an extent, of (new) fascism as well. Inscribing Rosenberg's claims on myth and types in a broader genealogy that goes from Romanticism all the way back to classical antiquity, in Plato's thought, the philosophers show that Rosenberg is reloading a conception of myth that rests on what Lacoue-Labarthe calls "typography," by which he means the formative power of mythic figures or types to impress their seal or form on that malleable material that is a subject, a people, a nation.[35]

Myth, just like mimesis, does not simply represent fictional realities; it also forms real people. Thus, extending a problematic inaugurated in "Typography," but with Rosenberg's section on "Myth and Type" in the foreground, Lacoue-Labarthe and Nancy write: "Myth is a fiction, in the strong, active sense of 'fashioning' [*façonnement*] . . . it is, therefore, a *fictioning* [*fictionnement*], whose role is to propose if not to impose, models or types . . . types in imitation of which an individual, or a city, or an entire people, can grasp [*saisir*] themselves and identify themselves."[36] Myth, again like mimesis, can, of course, have both negative or positive formative effects, for its *pathos* can generate both pathologies and patho-*logies*, depending on the models or types one imitates.[37] But the point here is that myth and mimesis are two sides of the same coin, for it is through the medium of myth that a mimetic identification with a type is triggered.

To be sure, Lacoue-Labarthe's and Nancy's *political* evaluation of this mimetic phenomenon in "The Nazi Myth" is radically opposed to Rosenberg. In *La fiction du politique*, Lacoue-Labarthe will caution readers: "One should not attribute to me the position I am analyzing."[38] Instead, the philosophers' *diagnostic* of the logic of fascism both mirrors and inverses Rosenberg's account of mythic types in a sense that is at least double, for it accounts for the emergence of both real and dreamed figures.

On the side of reality, contra Rosenberg, Lacoue-Labarthe and Nancy critique this *political* recuperation of myth for anti-Semitic and nationalist purposes so as to unmask the idea driving this fascist ideology as a pathological fable, but with Rosenberg they agree *theoretically* that the "greatest man" or "figures" are the "most powerful Myth shaping" insofar as they have the willpower to "dream" what Rosenberg calls "essential unity," "type," or "form" that will allow the Germans to "become what [they] are."[39] On the side of the dream, the philosophers contra Rosenberg firmly oppose the idea that Jews "dream of world domination" (they will reply, in another article, that the "Jewish People Do Not Dream").[40] But they also agree *with* Rosenberg that Germany's mythic unity is achieved by reawakening "primal dreams" that "have been lost and forgotten" but that the *Germans* have "begun to dream again."[41]

On both sides of the fiction and political divide, which as we have seen is far from impermeable, "The Nazi Myth" shows that it is from an identification with these types and the belief in national dreams they promote that myth, understood as formative and thus mimetic power, can be most powerfully reloaded.

This also means that in Rosenberg we find a confirmation of Lacoue-Labarthe's and Nancy's first proposition concerning the power of myth: namely, that the problem Nazism, and by extension (new) fascism as well, is confronting is first and foremost "a problem of *identity*." That is, an identity that lacks unity and is in need of a form, figure, or *Gestalt* embodied in mythic leaders or types who have the power to mediate what the philosophers call "the realization of the singular identity conveyed by the dream." And they add: "A belief, an immediate, unreserved adhesion to the dreamed figure is necessary for the myth to be what it is, or, if this may be said, for the form to take form [*pour que la figure prenne figure*]."[42]

Fascist and Nazi types, then, convoke the logic of myth and the dream they animate in order to provide an identity to a people that is dispossessed of proper being. For Lacoue-Labarthe and Nancy, this was true of the old Nazi myth and the types it generated in the wake of a characteristically German dispossession of identity that led to the most horrific crime against humanity in the history of the West—what Lacoue-Labarthe, echoing Conrad's "mythic" tale, *Heart of Darkness*, also calls "the horror of the West."[43] And echoing Girard, he will define this horror as "a sort of gigantic sacrificial politics with reformative aims."[44]

It is of course tempting to confine such horrors to the past. And should such horrors return, history is unlikely to repeat itself in the same way since new means of mass extermination are now available. And yet, as the threat of nuclear wars remains real, and as Girard foresaw, risks to "escalate to extremes," we should remain on guard. We are in fact beginning to realize that if not the horrors themselves, the new fascist types that are currently arising on the far right, most visibly in the United States and in Europe but also beyond the boundaries of the West. They might serve similar pathological functions in the wake of an economic, political, and environmental crisis that marks the dawn of the twenty-first century.

This is true at the level of both *what* these types say (*logos*) and *how* they say it (*lexis*). Let us briefly dissociate these two related aspects.

On the one hand, myth is currently reloaded at the level of the *content* of (new) fascist rhetoric as is made manifest in the number of types that promote an ontology of sameness in place of difference at the heart of Western dreams: hypernationalism, racism, sexism, phallocentrism, homophobia, Islamophobia, authoritarianism, and all these isms entail—scapegoating of minorities, exploitation of the working class, dismantling of public services, aggressive militarism, religious discrimination, erection of boundaries, anti-immigration policies, subordination of science to myth, anti-environmentalism, and so on. The list is long, the logic of pathos and terror it implies visible, and there is no doubt that a problem of identity still plays a prominent role in reloading the contagious power that informs what Connolly also calls a "type of mimesis grounded in narcissistic leadership."[45]

On the other hand, it is at the level of the *form* of fascist dreams that mythic power is most effectively deployed both by old and new fascist types on the political scene. As Lacoue-Labarthe and Nancy remind us, again with Rosenberg clearly in mind, myth should not be confused with the mythological, just as mimetic *pathoi* or affects should not be confused with mimetic representations. This is why they say that "Myth is a power more than it is a thing, an object, or a representation." And they add: "Mythical power is the power of the dream, of the projection of an image with which one identifies." Mythic power, then, is "an instrument of *identification*," or better, it is "*the* mimetic instrument par excellence," put to patho-*logical* use by authoritarian figures to generate the contagious *pathos* typical of (new) fascism.[46]

Typically, what was true for the old fascism continues to be true for the new fascism as well. As Trump hyperbolically puts it in his account of the dream, triggering the phenomenon he apparently represents: "The rallies became massive. The crowds were unbelievable. The enthusiasm was based on pure love. . . . The media, the politicians and the so-called leaders of our country reacted in horror."[47] The rhetorical style is comic when silently read, but the horror it generates when dramatically enacted via mimetic speeches is tragically real and, for the heterogeneous reasons we have discussed in previous chapters, effectively contaminating. While not the same as Nazism,[48] this disquieting mass phenomenon is a manifestation of what Lacoue-Labarthe and Nancy define as "Hitlerism"—namely, "the modern masses' openness to myth."[49]

The diagnostic of myth based on the distinction between content and form, *logos* and *lexis* is of Platonic inspiration, but Lacoue-Labarthe and Nancy supplement the ancient language of mimesis with the modern one of "identification" operating a shift from philosophy to psychoanalysis. Lacoue-Labarthe and Nancy rely, in fact, on their previous work on Freud and Lacan to define the power of mythic figures to cast a spell on the masses in terms of what Freud, in his most political book, *Group Psychology and Analysis of the Ego*, calls "identification," understood as the desire "to *be*" the other[50]—what Mikkel Borch-Jacobsen, also à partir de Lacoue-Labarthe and Girard, calls "*the* fundamental concept, or *Grundbegriff* of psychoanalysis."[51]

This tendency to identification, as Wilhelm Reich also recognized in *The Mass Psychology of Fascism*, "is the psychological basis of national narcissism, that is, of a self-confidence based on identification with the 'greatness of the nation.'"[52] If we also recall Lacan's emphasis on the ego's imaginary assumption of an *imago* or *Gestalt* during "the mirror stage," and the forms of *méconnaissance* it generates, it is clear that this psychoanalytical tradition, which in-*forms* mythic identification with a dream image, as Lacoue-Labarthe and Nancy understand it, has not lost any of its power today. Quite the contrary.

And yet, the philosophers' genealogy of myth reaches further back into the past as it adds a mimetic, bodily, and contagious supplement that opens an alternative, more embodied door to the unconscious that has mimetic pathos as a *via regia*. Thus, they specify that the "energy" or "force" of this identification is rooted in what they call "the Dionysian experience, as described by Nietzsche."[53] This second insight gets us closer to the accursed power of (new) fascist pathos to cast a spell on the population.

We have already discussed the importance of this genealogical link in relation to community; we now still need to unpack its relevance for our account of myth. There is, in fact, a deft, complex, and destabilizing inversion of perspectives at play in this reframing of the power of myth in terms of both *visual* (or Apollonian) mimesis and *bodily* (or Dionysian) mimesis that inverts Rosenberg's (Nordic) account of myth, complicates psychoanalytical accounts of unconscious identification, and generates doubling patho-*logical* effects that reach into the present.

Their overturning move is double and can be summarized in two mirroring points. First, Rosenberg, as we have seen, ties the problematic of myth to the one of types to account for the top-down vertical power of racist impressions of figures onto the racial soul. Lacoue-Labarthe and Nancy, on the other hand, invert perspectives by considering the problematic of mythic power from the angle of the mimetic crowd that identifies with such types to have an identity. Mythic power is thus mimetic in the sense that it rests on a desire "to be" a subject via an imaginary visual identification with what Lacoue-Labarthe, echoing Rosenberg but with Heidegger and Lacan in mind, calls image, figure or *Gestalt*; Nietzsche, following a classical terminology, calls these forms "representations," "phantoms, or dream images."[54] Mythic power is thus mimetic power in the sense that it is visual, aesthetic, and formative, that is, *Apollonian* power.

Second, Rosenberg advocates types that originate in

Greek and Roman culture, celebrates "light over darkness," and, borrowing Nietzsche's categories but fundamentally betraying his thought, celebrates an identification with the Greek (read Nordic) Apollo over and *against* the racial and psychic "deterioration" imported from the East by Dionysus.[55] Thus, in this racist reconstruction of *The Birth of Tragedy*, he says: "Foreign barbarians [followers of Dionysus] became Athenians, much as in our era, eastern Jews became German."[56] On the other hand, Lacoue-Labarthe and Nancy, contra Rosenberg, trace a genealogy of German rituals back to what they call the "savage Greece of group rituals," in which Dionysian *pathos* furnishes "the *identifying force*" that has the power to reload myth in the twentieth century.[57] Mythic power is thus mimetic power, in the sense that it is dramatic, intoxicating, and transgressive—that is, *Dionysian* power.

"The Nazi Myth" is here facing *The Myth of the 20th Century*. And in this mirroring confrontation between Apollonian and Dionysian principles, a certain conception of myth is reborn out of a mimetic unconscious that, as should be clear by now, casts a shadow on the twenty-first century as well. This unconscious has mimesis as a *via regia*, for it oscillates, pendulum-like, between competing mimetic principles: visual identification (or dreams) and affective contagion (or frenzy); the formal language of *imago* and *Gestalt* characteristic of Apollonian forms (or representations) and the formless language of affect and *pathos* characteristic of Dionysian force (or impersonation).

Now, both Apollonian and Dionysian principles are at play in the birth of tragedy, as Nietzsche understands it, and both principles inform the birth of the Nazi myth, as Lacoue-Labarthe and Nancy interpret it. Still, their destabilizing mirroring move opens up an alternative path to the labyrinth of mythic power that still needs to be fully pursued. Namely, that in its affective force or power, myth can never be fully contained in a unitary, stabilizing, homogeneous form, figure, or *Gestalt* represented from a visual distance. If only because the Apollonian image or type that triggers dreams and elicits mythic identification generates a frenzy that always leaks in bodily, destabilizing, Dionysian experiences. That is, heterogeneous experiences that, as Georges Bataille also recognized, transgress the boundaries of individuation generating feelings of "attraction of repulsion" constitutive of the "psychological structure of fascism."[58]

Put differently, in imaginary fictions it may be possible to contain the Dionysian *pathos* of fascist types within a psychoanalytic notion of identification with an *imago* that erects the illusion of a unitary form in Apollonian dreams constitutive of the Nazi myth. And yet, in political practice, the emergence of new fascist movements urges genealogists of myth to invert the *telos* of this reading and unmask the apparent unity of this Apollonian form or dream as a *méconnaissance*. That is, a misrecognition that underneath the unitary *imago* flows a formless Dionysian *pathos* characteristic of a mimetic unconscious that triggers affective currents of intoxication contagion. For it is ultimately via such hypnotic, mimetic, and contagious movements that the "identifying force" or "power" of myth is constantly reloaded. In short, new fascist power is, at its source, Dionysian power, for it is formless, affective, and intoxicating will to power.

Does this mean that the leader figure is as formless and improper as the crowd that mimics him? And what side of mimesis mediates his mythic will to power? The power of the dream image in paving the way for mythic identification should not be underestimated, especially in a mass-mediatized, digital culture characterized by mimetic, or better hypermimetic simulations that represent dreams—dreams of greatness that are attainable only for the few in reality, but that cast a hypnotic spell on the many disenfranchised working-class subjects who identify with virtual fictions to compensate for the failed attainment of the dream.

From professional success to economic power, entrepreneurial individualism to white-nationalist sentiments, phallocentric exploitation of women to narcissistic media celebrity, freedom to hire in political fictions and fire in fictional realities, it is clear that mythic identifications with typical simulations of the dream were already unconsciously at play in fictional images before they reappeared on the political stage in reality. They triggered a redoubled enthusiasm among a formless, malleable, and rather divided mass qua public afflicted by real social grievances, but also programmed, from childhood on, to identify with "heroic" dream figures.

In this Apollonian sense, such types erect a narcissistic, unitary image that elicits a virtual identification with a typical manifestation of the dream. This dream is an illusory representation, form, or "simulation of sovereignty" that not only dissolves the shadow-line between truth and lies but also reloads old phantoms via new media generated by a technical, or better, digital revolution that has the "hypermimetic" power of turning real politics into a political fiction.[59] As Lacoue-Labarthe and Nancy notice, "the problem of myth is always indissociable from that of art";[60] the former goes as far as saying that "the essence of the political is to be sought in art"[61]—which does not mean that this art needs to be "Great Art," or even "good" art.

Still, this aesthetization of politics, or "national-aestheticism" (*national-esthétisme*), as Lacoue-Labarthe calls it, cuts both ways, for its visual (Apollonian) efficacy ultimately rests on less visible but quite intoxicating (Dionysian) pathos. An identification with images, in fact, tends to rest on collective rituals that trigger massive doses of affective and contagious reactions that are formless in nature, chthonic in origins, and follow Dionysian principles that are constitutive of the mimetic unconscious, if only because this unconscious has the figure of the actor, or mime, as the all-too-human medium to reload enthusiastic outbreaks on political stages, both real and virtual.

Dramatic manifestations of the mimetic unconscious include the use of gestures rather than words, *pathos* rather than *logos*, facial mimicry, dramatic poses, impersonations, histrionic expressions, but also aggressive accusations, the incitement to violence, the terror of nuclear escalations, not to speak of the phallocentric scandals, the lurid sexual fantasies, and other abject subject matters that, as Bataille was quick to sense, are not simply external to the psychology of fascism but are constitutive of its transgressive patho-*logy*, endowing fascist leaders without proper qualities with an energetic charge, or Dionysian discharge, that is nolens volens constitutive of political nightmares.

The Apprentice President Unmasked

The genealogical detour via contagious crowds, communal movements, and mythic identification, then, brings us back to the mimetic, theatrical principles with which we started. But in the process, it also offers a Nietzschean supplement that identifies emerging protean types on the political scene. In the context of a critique of actors turned masters in *Gay Science*, Nietzsche offers the following diagnostic of mimetic principles we should now be in a position, if not to fully contain, at least to partially unmask:

> Falseness with a good conscience; the delight in simulation exploding as a power that pushes aside one's so-called "character," flooding it and at times extinguishing it; the inner craving for a role and mask, for *appearance*; an excess of the capacity for all kinds of adaptations that can no longer be satisfied in the service of the most immediate and narrowest utility—all of this is perhaps not only peculiar to the actor?[62]

And thus, we may add, of the (new) fascist leader? Especially since, as Nietzsche—in a diagnostic phrase that we can now hear in its heterogeneous mimetic ramifications—was quick to sense the dawn of a world in which "the 'actors,' *all* kinds of actors, become the real masters."[63]

Following the twists and turns of such an "actor" qua "master" makes us see that this phantom figure may be a type, as Rosenberg suggested, and the type will appear to give form to a divided people without a proper identity, as Lacoue-Labarthe and Nancy indicated. But it is important to specify these claims by saying that this type or figure is not singular but plural; it is not unitary and rigid, but protean and plastic. As we have seen, this protean figure that is now occupying the leading role on the political stage visibly relies on "falseness," "simulation," "appearance," and "an excess of the capacity for all kinds of adaptations." In the process, he gives voice to hypernationalist, racist, and militarist tendencies constitutive of the myth of greatness that is attainable for the few, yet generates mass enthusiasm in the many as well. Why? For the patho-logical reasons we have outlined so far but also because the powers of mimesis

and lies is as old as the origins of mimetic theory, but the emergence of new media is currently reloading the power of myth in terms that repeatedly urge us to look back in order to better see what lies ahead. Let us thus recall that Plato, in book 7 of *The Republic*, paints a picture of subjects tied at the bottom of a cave who are born in bondage: "Prevented by the fetters from turning their heads," Socrates says, they are forced to look at "puppet shows" that are merely the "shadows cast from the fire on the wall of the cave that fronted them" (514a–515a). Such subjects, Socrates continues, "would deem reality to be nothing else than the shadows of artificial objects" (515c), appearances without substance, phantoms removed from reality.

Since Plato, this suggestive allegory has been applied to all kinds of mimetic spectacles—from the theater to the cinema and, we should add, new media—to indicate the power of mythic shadows to mask the truth and promote lies. That is certainly its most visible function, but there is another, less-visible, but no less insidious mimetic function that urges us to ask: what if these shadows that are cast on the wall of representation cast a spell on the ego as well? Or better, couldn't we say that it is because these subjects are under the spell of an endless puppet show, magnetized by the spectacle, not in conscious possession of their ego, that these shadows appear real in the first place?

What is certain is that the myth, and the Janus-faced conception of visual/affective mimesis it entails, has not lost its relevance in the digital age. On the contrary, since we are literally born in all-surrounding media environments that stage all kinds of shows, the allegory has become a reality. We are subterranean creatures living in a world of shadows—and the exit of the cavern is increasingly out of reach. In fact, the master of the show counters those who attempt to unmask the puppets by setting up a mirror that denounces real facts as "fake news." This is a simple but effective, hypermimetic technique. It generates an endless mirroring effect that absorbs all critiques in the logic they are opposing. If it makes access to the "true world" impossible, it is not the ideal, transcendental world of Platonic Forms that is in question, but the factual, material world on which interpretations should rest that is currently vanishing.

Nietzsche, whose name is often tied to interpretations rather than facts, might not appear to be an ideal ally to unmask this puppet show. Especially since in a famous passage in *Twilight of the Idols* that recapitulates the history of Western metaphysics from Plato to the present, he celebrated the abolition of the "'true' world." For Nietzsche, there is, in fact, no "true," ideal world of Forms that would reduce the material, phenomenal world to a mere shadow, appearance, or phantom. And in a passage that has generated much enthusiasm in postmodern quarters, he adds: "With the true world we have abolished the apparent one."[64] To be sure, when it comes to *metaphysical fictions*, Nietzsche celebrates this moment as "noon," the moment of the "briefest shadow."[65] And yet, in an inversion of perspectives that is perfectly in line with his severe condemnation of the actor, when it comes to *political realities* he could as well have denounced this moment as twilight: the moment of the longest shadow.[66]

Either way, this is the liminal moment we are in. As the shadow of (new) fascism is cast on the present, the effect is double, as it is both epistemic and psychological. On the one hand, an endless game of mirroring effects makes it increasingly difficult to distinguish between truth and lies, realities and shadows, original facts and alternative facts— moment of the briefest shadow, loss of original facts, incipit of the apprentice president show; on the other hand, the dramatic scene casts such a hypnotic spell on the chained subjects who forget the real chain, suspend disbelief, and enjoy the pathos generated by the puppet show—moment of the longest shadow, loss of an original ego, return of the phantom of the ego.

What is new, then, in the age of hypermimesis is not only the generation of illusory shadows that are mistaken for reality (mimesis)—for that strategy was, albeit in less pervasive ways, part of old fascism as well. Nor solely that these shadows bring new virtual realities into being that do not have anything to do with reality (simulations)—for such hyperreal simulations still pose the question of their relation to reality and truth. What is new in the politics of (new) fascism is that these hyperreal shadows generate material mimetic effects in the real world in terms that shift the attention from a visual search for truth behind the shadows to an *affective* demand for pathos on the side of an ego that has itself turned into a shadow or phantom of the ego (hypermimesis).

From this perspective, spectators of new fascist political shows are reduced to phantom figures chained to an all-pervasive, endless, and deplorable spectacle, caught up in a chain of dramas they are magnetized to follow. The driving force here is not to detect any reality behind the Apollonian shadow but to experience the transgressive Dionysian affects it generates instead. Myth, as Plato, Nietzsche, Girard, Lacoue-Labarthe, and other mimetic theorists well understood, is effective in spreading affects like fear, anger, desire, jealousy, resentment, vengeance that operate on the irrational side of the soul—what we call the mimetic unconscious; and these are also the affects new fascist leaders can mobilize to manipulate masses and publics via new media that turn virtual shadows into psychic realities—what we call hypermimesis. Or, to use traditional aesthetic categories, the power of myth reloaded on (new) media by fictional leaders qua actors generates a willing suspension of disbelief central to experiencing tragic pleasure—a pleasure that does not generate a cathartic purification but a contagious addiction to sacrificial dramas instead.

Once this affective demand for mythic spectacles is injected in the sphere of politics, it is difficult to counter the leaders that provide the daily show on which the news has come to rely. Paradoxically, even those television shows that are critical of apprentice presidents and attempt to break the spell of mythic shadows risk, by virtue of their use of the same media, unwittingly contributing to the success of the accursed leaders they focus on day and night.

Take satirical television shows, for instance. On the one hand, as I point out in the interview that follows this chapter, comedians are ideally placed to critique new fascist figures as phantasmal appearances without substance. In fact, they rely on the same dramatic skills as the apprentice president to unmask his lies, while at the same time offering a factually informed, satirical, and intelligent view of American politics that is far superior to so-called real news on partisan television channels like *Fox News*. On the other hand, by virtue of their use of the same media, ultimately these shows find themselves paradoxically contributing additional episodes to the Trump daily show in at least two ways. First, by ca-thecting viewers' attention on the protagonist of a political fiction in general and on his latest scandal in particular at the expense of other, perhaps less spectacular but equally important news. And second, by generating an affective demand, or rather, addiction, for the very political scandals their shows so effectively critique.[67]

Lastly, the efficacy of mimesis takes another twist via the digital turn. Neither good nor bad in itself, the Internet can be put to both fascist and anti-fascist use in theory; yet, in recent years, it played a key role in the rise of new leaders inclined to fascism in political practice. The interactive na-ture of new social media has, in fact, a spiraling effect that further reloads the mythic power of hypermimesis. While providing the illusion of active participation, these social media are efficacious means to promote fascist myths of greatness and racial superiority, and disseminate lies on a massive scale for a number of reasons I schematically outline before concluding.

First, new social media like Facebook and Twitter contribute to the flow of "breaking news" that saturates daily lives, generating addictions to mythic spectacles on which (new) fascist leaders thrive. Second, they dissolve the boundary between public and private life by making politics the subject of daily life. Third, they subject the population directly to power by exposing users to daily presidential tweets that are perceived, paradoxically, both as personal messages and as massively shared messages—a doubling that amplifies the hypnotic power of the medium. Fourth, the increasing number of people who rely on Facebook for their news radically diminishes the field of vision, makes them vulnerable to views that—via algorithms that target users with personalized information—reinforce already held ideological beliefs, increase somnambulism, and open the way for massive forms of cyber-manipulation that are, as I write, under investigation and will require further analysis.

At this stage, what is clear is that the power of myth is no longer limited to presidential, nationalist, or even human influences. Surrounded by shadows, manipulated by affects, open to cyberattacks, influenced by algorithms, the hyper-mimetic subject chained to new media from childhood on can be dispossessed of its ego, put in a permanent state of light hypnotic trance, and effectively programmed to act against its "personal" interests. The media are indeed *new* and open up disconcerting new forms of mass manipulation, but their power to cast a spell on the ego rests on a human, very human vulnerability to mimetic dispossessions. Once we are under the spell of phantoms, turning away from the show in order to see the figures responsible for top-down projections of fluttering shadows in reality is not an idea that comes naturally.

And yet—and this is the point with which I would like to conclude—this does not mean that alternative perspectives cannot be culturally promoted. In writing this book I have been motivated by the hope that a diagnostic of (new) fascism that sits on the shoulders of an old mimetic tradition can join the chorus of dissenting voices that are currently urging us to look at the show from a critical distance in order to see the (hyper)mimetic mechanisms that reproduce it. These joint efforts urge us to slow down the show's movement, cast light on the shadows, and diagnose their hypnotic (will to) to power as a pathology in need of cure.

They might also make us see that the chains do not tie us to fictional shows alone; they also connect us to real people whose bondage we share. If we shift our perspective, we might also feel that collectively, our freedom of movement, and thus of thought, and thus of action, is greater than we might realize. Who knows? Perhaps an old mimetic medium that, in the past, has not been deprived of performative effects in real life might serve as a link in a chain of thinkers that can help us unmask the shady mime, reveal the source of his mythic power, and promote real political alternatives, from the bottom up.

What is certain is that this phantom is, strictly speaking, *improper*, in a double conceptual/literal sense: on the conceptual side, it lacks proper, essential qualities that would guarantee an identity, even a dreamed, apparent, and fictional identity; on the literal side, it is also improper in the most basic sense of being inappropriate, unacceptable, illegitimately dramatizing the protean qualities of an old actor—playing the new role of an apprentice president.

Coda
Fascism Now and Then:
William Connolly and Nidesh Lawtoo in Conversation

William Connolly and I started discussing emerging (new) fascist movements back in the spring of 2016, at Johns Hopkins University. Donald Trump's campaign was beginning to gain traction in the primaries and, as I mentioned in the introduction, we shared a concern with the affective and contagious power of his rhetoric. As we had the occasion to meet again, a year later, this time in Weimar, Germany, in the summer of 2017, we naturally resumed the conversation. We had kept in regular touch, and while I had written a few articles on new fascism, Connolly was at work on a short book titled *Aspirational Fascism*—we were already into material, so to speak.

Since Connolly's book has appeared in the meantime, I thought it would be useful to conclude this study by including our conversation on what fascism was in the past and what it is becoming now—a way of joining forces, establishing some genealogical connections, and closing the circle.

Nidesh Lawtoo (NL): You are a political theorist, but the kind of theory you are interested in is entangled with a number of different disciplines, from continental philosophy to anthropology, sociology to literary theory, stretching to include in-depth dialogues with hard sciences such as biology, geology, and the neurosciences. Across these disciplines you are known for your work on pluralism, for your critique of secularism, and for a conception of agonistic democracy that is inscribed in a Nietzschean philosophical tradition.

In your recent work, you have opened up this materialist tradition to the question of the Anthropocene. I am thinking of *The Fragility of Things* (2013) and, more recently, *Facing the Planetary* (2017). At the same time, in the wake of the 2016 presidential election in the United States, or actually already prior to it, you have been folding these future-oriented concerns with the planetary back into the all-too-human fascist politics that was constitutive of the 1930s and 1940s in Europe, but that is currently returning to cast a shadow on the contemporary scene in Europe and, closer to home, in the United States.

Genealogy of Fascism

NL: As a response to this emerging political threat, last semester (spring 2017) you taught a graduate seminar at Johns Hopkins titled "What Was/Is Fascism?," which I would like to take as a springboard to frame our discussion. This title suggests at least two related observations: first, that fascism is a political reality that is not only related to the past of other nations but remains a threat for the present of our own nations as well; and second, that in order to understand what fascism is today, it is necessary to adopt genealogical lenses and inscribe new fascist movements in a tradition of thought aware of what fascism was in the 1920s and 1930s.

So, my first questions are: What are some of the main lessons that emerged from this genealogy of fascism? And what is "new" about this reemergence of authoritarian, neo-fascist, or as you call them, "aspirational fascist" leaders that are now haunting the contemporary political scene?

Bill Connolly (BC): That's a good summary of what I am trying to do and of how this problematic on "What Was/Is Fascism" has emerged. Maybe the best way for me to start is to say that if you try to do a genealogy of Fascism your focus is on the present; the first thing that you pay close attention to is not just how things were, say, in German Nazism or in Italian Fascism, but also how comparisons to those very different situations may help us to focus on new strains and dangers today.[1]

Another aspect of a genealogy of Fascism is to sharpen our thinking about what positive possibilities to pursue in the present. Current temptations to a new kind of Fascism might encourage us to rethink some classic ideals anti-Fascists pursued in the past, asking how they succumbed then and what their weaknesses might have been. Some opponents of Fascism were inspired by liberalism, others by neo-liberalism, and others yet by smooth ideals of collectivism or communalism. So, a genealogy of Fascism can help us to rethink ideals articulated in the past, testing their relative powers as antidotes to Fascism. And it can point to pressures that encourage advocates of other ideals to go over to Fascism. That's part of what I hoped we could begin to do in this seminar.

Moving to the second part of the question: what are the dangers in the present that make some of us hear eerie echoes from the past? Well, a huge omission has been created in the Euro-American world, especially in the United States, where my focus is concentrated. The neoliberal Right has succeeded in pushing concentrations of wealth and income to an ever-smaller group of tycoons at the top, while the pluralizing Left—which I have actively supported over the last forty years—has had precarious (and highly variable) success in its efforts to advance the standing of African Americans, Hispanics, women, diverse sexualities, and several religious faiths. There is much more to be done on these fronts, to be sure, particularly with respect to African Americans.

But one minority placed in a bind between these two opposing drives—and the rhetorics that have sustained each—has been the white working and lower-middle class. Portions of it have taken revenge for this neglect, first, in joining the evangelical/capitalist resonance machine that really got rolling in the early 1980s, and now in being tempted by the aspirational Fascism of Donald Trump. That has created happy hunting grounds for a new kind of neo-Fascist movement, one that would extend white triumphalism; intimidate the media; attack Muslims, Mexicans, and independent women; perfect the use of Big Lies; suppress minority voting; allow refugee pressures to grow as the effects of the Anthropocene accelerate; sacrifice diplomacy to dangerous military excursions; and displace science and the professoriate as independent centers of knowledge and public authority.

So, that is where I want to place my focus: working upon earlier ideals of democratic pluralism to respond to this emerging condition. When I say emerging condition, I don't mean that success is inevitable—the multiple forces of resistance are holding so far. I mean a set of powerful pressures on the horizon that must be engaged before it could become too late to forestall them.

NL: On this question of emerging conditions, you and I share a concern with the rhetoric neo-fascist leaders like Donald Trump have mobilized to win the election, an affective and infective rhetoric that many of us in academia might have been tempted to downplay or dismiss for its apparent simplicity and crudeness—at least during the electoral campaign. But it has worked in the past and continues to be working in the present too.

In light of this genealogical reminder, we both argue that critics and theorists on the left need to be much more attentive to the ways in which this fascist rhetoric—based on repetition, use of images rather than ideas, spectacular lies, but also gestures, facial expressions, incitation to violence, racist and sexist language, nationalism, and so on—operates on what I call the "mimetic unconscious" and you call the "visceral register of cultural life."

The fascist "art of persuasion" is not based on rational arguments, political programs, or even basic facts. Rather, its aim is to trigger affective reactions that, as some precursors of fascist psychology (I'm thinking of Gustave Le Bon and Gabriel Tarde, but also Nietzsche, Bataille, Girard, among others I started discussing in *The Phantom of the Ego*) also noticed, have the power to spread contagiously, especially in a crowd, but now also in publics watching such spectacles from a virtual distance. Could you say more about the affective power of this rhetoric, especially in light of a type of politics that increasingly operates in the mode of fictional entertainment?

BC: That's a really big question and it's at the center of what I would like to try to do, however imperfectly. In preparation for this seminar, I read, for the first time in my life, Hitler's *Mein Kampf*. We explored huge sections of it in class, and I noted that at first no students wanted to present on this book. I also noted that almost no one I talked to, in the U.S. and Germany (we're having this interview in Weimar, Germany), had read that book either. The book was in large part dictated by Hitler to Rudolf Hess, while they were in prison together in the early 1920s. It reads as a text that could have been spoken: the rhythms, the punchiness, the tendency to lapse into diatribes in a way people sometimes do when they are talking. . . .

What Hitler says in the book is that he spent much of his early life in politics rehearsing how to be an effective mass speaker: practicing larger-than-life gesticulations, pugnacious facial expressions, theatrical arm and body movements on stage to punctuate key phrases. The phrase/body combos in his speeches—we watched a few speeches—are thrown like punches: a left jab, a right jab, a couple more punches, and then boom—a knockout punch thrown to the audience! They are punches. Speech as a mode of attack; speech as communication set on the register of attack. Now acts of violence do not become big jumps for leaders or followers. In fact, as Hitler says, he welcomed violence at his rallies. His guards, who later became storm troopers, would rush in and mercilessly beat up protestors, doing so to incite the crowd to a higher pitch of passion.

If we think about Hitler's speaking style in relation to Trump's, it may turn out that Hitler was right about one thing: the professoriate pay attention mostly to writing; not nearly enough to the powers of diverse modes of speech.

Of course, there are exceptions: Judith Butler is one and there are others. But writing and texts are what academics love to attend to, and styles of speech require a different kind of attention. If you *read* one of Trump's speeches it may look incoherent, but it has its own coherence when delivered to a crowd. He also may rehearse those theatrical gestures and grimaces, walking back and forth on stage, circling around while pointing to the crowd to draw its acclaim, and so forth.

When you attend to his speaking style, you see that he has introduced a mode of communication that speaks to simmering grievances circulating in those crowds. Of course, he speaks to other constituencies too, some of them the super-rich. But the speeches are pitched to one prime constituency. His rhetoric and gestures tap, accelerate, and amplify those grievances as he seeks to channel them in a specific direction. Immigrants are responsible for deindustrialization, he says, never noting automation and free corporate tickets to desert the towns and cities that had housed and subsidized them so generously.

When Trump engages in the Big Lie scenario, which

forms a huge part of his speeches and tweets, followers do not always believe the lies. Rather, they accept them as *pegs* upon which to hang their grievances. So, when journalists ask, "Do you believe that he is going to build the wall and Mexico will pay for it?" many say, "No, I don't believe that." But when he says it, they yell and scream anyway because the promise is connected to their grievances.

Trump is the most recent practitioner of the Big Lie perfected by Hitler earlier. Of course, the latter's Biggest Lie was the assertion that Jews were themselves master demagogues of the Big Lie. That is exactly how Donald Trump transfigures the production of Fake News on right-wing blogs; he charges CNN and the media in general with being purveyors of Fake News. The strategy of reversal is designed to make people doubt the veracity of all claims brought to them, preparing them to accept those that vent their grievances the most.

We have to understand how the Big Lie scenario works, what kinds of grievances it amplifies, how apparent incoherences in Trump's speeches provide collection points to intensify grievances and identify vulnerable scapegoats—until people leave his speeches electrified and ready to go. They are excited when guards usher a protester roughly off the premises. As the crowd screams, Trump says: "Don't you love my rallies?" Those on the pluralist and egalitarian Left have to learn how this dynamic works, rather than merely saying, "Those people are stupid if they believe those Big Lies." That plays into Trump's hands.

As to how the intertext between entertainment and politics grows, well, Trump was in entertainment as well as being a mogul in real estate, where appearances and staging make up a large part of the show. Moreover, his Atlantic City investments pulled him closer to criminal elements, and he deploys gangster-like tactics to cajole and threaten people. He moves back and forth between these venues. He is not the first one to have done so. Reagan did too. But Trump has perfected a new version of these exchanges, reinforced by blogs and tweets.

rhetorical alternatives that open up space for resistance, dissent, and political action.

Within this configuration, and to reframe my previous question on the relation between fascist politics and entertainment, what do you think of the role a genre such as political satire or comedy plays as a counter-rhetorical strategy? As a non-U.S. citizen who has lived in the United States during several presidential elections, I noticed how this genre is center stage in American politics, to an extent people from other countries might even have trouble imagining: From *The Daily Show* to *The Tonight Show*, *The Late Show* to *The Saturday Night Live Show*, to the *Last Week Tonight Show*, and many other shows that inform a big segment of the U.S. population—in ways that, I must say, are often more accurate and perceptive than so-called real news, like *Fox News*.

In a way, comedians seem ideally placed not only to understand but also to unmask and oppose Trump's rhetoric on his own terrain. By training and profession, actors rely on rhetorical skills that derive from the world of performance and operate on an affective, bodily, and mimetic register. And they do so in order to counter, horizontally, the vertical rhetoric of fascism—though I noticed their reluctance to use the word "fascism" in their shows—for that, genealogists are perhaps still needed . . . Anyway, I find it telling that specialists of dramatic impersonation (or actors) are now those who, paradoxically, unmask the fictions of political celebrities (or actors).

I value the work done on that front and I pay attention to it, but as I watch some of these shows I also have a lingering ambivalence and concern I'd like to share with you. On the one hand, the rhetoric of satire effectively channels political grievances to unmask, via comedic strategies, the absurdity of the Big Lie scenario you describe, as well as other authoritarian symptoms (nepotism, dismantling of public services, racist and sexist actions, dismissal of science, etc.); on the other hand, comedy also seems to contribute to blurring the line between politics and fiction, generating an affective confusion of genres that could well be part of the problem, not the solution.

Of course, political satire has been around for a long time, but the promotion of politics as a form of mass-mediatized entertainment that saturates—via new media—all corners of private life is a recent phenomenon, and this fictionalization of politics, in turn, should perhaps redefine the critical role satire plays as well. In this spiraling loop, the laughter comedians generate wittily exposes political lies, counters docile subordinations to power, promotes freedom of speech, and perhaps, in small doses, even offers a temporary cathartic outlet that can be necessary for political activism.

And yet, at the same time, I also worry that comedy could generate an affective demand—I'm even tempted to say unhealthy addiction—precisely for those political scandals (the sexist language and actions, the lurid tapes, the spectacular firings, the secret investigations, and so on) it sets out to critique, leading an already media-dependent population to paradoxically focus political attention on the leader qua fictional celebrity to the detriment of real political action itself. What is your take on this double bind? And how do you evaluate these comedic efforts to rechannel a visceral/mimetic rhetoric contra (new) fascist leaders?

BC: I take an ambivalent approach to them, too. This is a very good question because my own perspective, which draws sustenance from your work on mimetic contagion in *The Phantom of the Ego*, is that certain kinds of stances that liberals often adopt, that deliberative theorists and others do too, in which you say that the visceral register of cultural life must be transcended. Modes of politics that demean analysis, policy, rational argument, and so forth are wrong-headed and have to be replaced. I too prize argument and truth.

But I also believe that there is never a vacuum on the visceral register of cultural life, that this register—which can be affectively rich and conceptually coarse—is ineliminable. Infants, you remind us, respond to the gestures, facial expressions, laughter, movements, and prompts of parents and siblings on the way to learning language, and this dimension of relational being never simply dies out. It constitutes the affective tone of life. But the visceral register can be engaged very differently than Trump does, as we move back and forth across the visceral and refined registers to pour an ethos of presumptive generosity into both.

If we do not become skilled at this, we open the door to authoritarians to fill the vacuum. Those of us on the left need to find alternative ways to allow the two registers to work back and forth on each other, to be part of each other, so that our most refined beliefs are filled with positive affective tonality and we are equipped to resist the Trumpian assaults. One thing neo-Fascist rhetoric teaches us is the ineliminability of the visceral level of cultural life.

Some comedians—when they show you in amusing ways, as *Saturday Night Live* comics and others do, how Trumpian rhetoric, rhythms, gestures, facial expressions, and demeanor work—imply that all this could be replaced with something entirely different. Well, it must be replaced, but not with something that denies the power of gesture and rhetoric, as those mirror neurons and olfactory sensors on our bodies absorb inflows below reflective attention. It is also necessary to examine how different sorts of bodily discipline encourage some modes of mimesis and discourage others. And so, I have an ambivalent relationship to comedians who do the exposés, depending on how they do it and what alternative they pursue.

The question is whether there are some who can carry us, as they show how the contagion works, to other rhetorical styles that don't deny the complexity of life and that help to infuse refined intellectual judgments with an ethos of presumptive generosity and courage across differences in identity, faith, and social position. These counter-possibilities, then, need to be part of the comedy acts. Sometimes I think that people like Sarah Silverman and Steve Colbert get this, while someone like the guy on *Saturday Night Live* may not. I'm glad that we've had these comedic interventions, so that people can look again at what is conveyed and how it is conveyed. But when responses take simply the form of name-calling, they incite more agitated segments of the white working and lower-middle classes and teach us nothing about how to woo them in a different direction.

It's a real quandary. Part of the reason, again, is that there is never a vacuum on the visceral register of being, neither for the constituencies that Trump courts nor for the intellectuals and pundits who seek to pull these forces in different directions. Trump's advantage is that it may be easier under conditions of social stress to drag people down than it is to lift them to a higher nobility. Cornel West, however, is a rhetorician who combines nobility, presumptive generosity, and courage against aspirational Fascism. Trump is one of crassness and cruelty.

The Ambivalences of Mimesis

BC: But now it's my turn to ask some questions. You have written the notes of ambivalence in mimesis, particularly perhaps Fascist mimesis. Could you say a bit more about how that ambivalence works and what effects it sometimes has—how modes of contagion that work for a while sometimes lose their power? This seems to be a crucial issue to engage today.

NL: Yes, absolutely crucial. And difficult to pinpoint, perhaps because of the ambivalences, or double movements, that mimesis tends to generate. Mimesis is usually translated as imitation, but since humans imitate in radically different ways, it's a notoriously difficult concept to define, which adds different layers to these ambivalences.

Schematically, mimesis can be linked to both representation and vision as well as to mimicry and affects. A realist painter is said to imitate or represent nature not unlike a realist novelist represents the world; but then a child also imitates his parents, a student his or her teachers (or, more probably, favorite movie stars), and people generally imitate figures they admire and who serve as models, good or bad. While the dominant tendency so far has been to translate mimesis in terms of representation, I'm interested in the behavioral, affective, and as you also say, contagious dimension of mimesis—what some call mimetism. Figures like Plato, Nietzsche, Tarde, Girard, Lacoue-Labarthe, Borch-Jacobsen, and others promote analogous views.

On the shoulders of this tradition, I like to remind my students that mimesis comes from *mimos* (mime or actor) and that is originally linked to theatrical skills like impersonation, mimicry, and bodily performance. My sense is that there is an enormous affective power at play in mimetic skills that can be put to political use, and abuse, especially in a culture that has turned politics into a form of spectacle. It's perhaps for this reason that actors turned politicians can cast such a spell on a significant segment of the population.

Mimesis is thus not always manifested as an image that we consciously see, but is constitutive of an environment that we feel with all our senses. We might not be fully conscious of it, especially if we're used to our environment, but it affects us nonetheless, and deeply so. A bit like the fish that is asked by the other fish, "how is the water today?" And it answers, surprised: "what's water?" Mimesis is the biocultural water we swim in: it's transparent, often imperceptible, and pervasive. Whether we like it or not, we're soaked in it, and the types of currents that surround us—from the family we're born into to the schools we attend, the friends we make and the profession we choose, the shows we watch to the people we follow online—have a strong mimetic influence on how we feel, think, act, and, eventually, vote. For better and worse.

So, to get to your question, there is indeed a political ambivalence at play in mimetic spells. Mimesis, and the affective contagion it generates, is most visible in the case of fascist leaders who use the skills of the actor to trigger aggressive nationalism, violent emotions, scapegoating mechanisms, military aggressions, etc., but it is always at play on political stages and can be used to generate positive emotions as well, such as sympathy, compassion, and solidarity.

There is, in fact, a fundamental political indeterminacy at play in mimesis in the sense that it can be put to both fascist and anti-fascist uses. It's a double-edged sword that cuts both ways. In both cases, I share your sense that it is the performative or mimetic register politicians rely on to generate identification (via gestures, tonality of voice, mimicry, etc.), which in turn is disseminated via all kinds of mass media, that has the power to generate the mass enthusiasm central to winning an election. I think this is one of the reasons we both started to worry about Trump early on in the campaign—as a showman of sorts, he mastered the mimetic register.

But your question about the ambivalence of fascist mimesis goes beyond well-established political oppositions between Left and Right. It's unpopular to say it, but I think it's important to acknowledge that, to different degrees, *we're all susceptible to the affective forces at play in fascist mimesis*. This is difficult territory because it implies recognizing that we're all vulnerable to mimetic emotions such as violence, fear, ressentiment, vengeance, especially in times of crisis. We might not be as autonomous, rational, and self-contained as we might like to think. Of course, it's always easier to see mimesis at work in others than in ourselves, and the challenge is more than doubled if what is at stake is the recognition of *fascist* mimesis.

In this sense, the term fascism we both chose to adopt to talk about present leaders that could simply be defined as populists, creates complications. As a culture, we have become so accustomed to thinking that fascism happened long ago, in totalitarian countries far away, and could not happen in our own democratic country. It's a mythic distinction but a powerful one.

At the same time, we are beginning to learn that fascism does not stop at national borders and often emerges from "democratic" processes within one's national walls. Using the terms like "(new) fascism" or "aspirational fascism"—with all the indeterminacies and potentialities they entail—might be strategically useful to help us remember the historical lesson attached to the second term. Namely, that we're all potentially vulnerable to fascism because we are all vulnerable to

If we're attentive to the mimetic currents we swim in, we can perhaps find strategies to swim in an opposed direction using *both* our reflective *and* mimetic faculties. Bataille spoke of the "attraction and repulsion" fascist leaders trigger in the crowd; Nietzsche used the notion of "pathos of distance" to designate a similar double movement. There might thus be a way of channeling the currents of visceral repulsion (new) fascist leaders generate to initiate modes of affective and reflective resistance and opposition to fascist mimesis.

While I fear that politics becoming entertainment intensifies this fascination for fascist pathos to an unprecedented degree, it's always possible to set up a distance from the dominant spectacle in which we bathe, and swim somewhere else. Regaining autonomy helps in theory—that's what Nietzsche sought in the Alps, away from crowds, and I have deep sympathy for that. But in practice, since many of us are mimetic creatures living in urban centers, it might be more effective to join others who are already engaged in anti-fascist movements, protests, and in the formation of alternative communities or assemblages. A different form of mimesis linked to sympathy, mutual respect, and solidarity can then not only be nurtured in such environments; the social environment retroacts mimetically on the ego and amplifies anti-fascist dispositions. And this, I think, brings me to your preference for swarms over crowds.

From the Crowd to the Swarm

NL: In your new book, *Facing the Planetary*, you have a chapter titled "The Politics of Swarming and the General Strike," which might make some readers wonder: what is the difference between a crowd and a swarm?

More specifically, in an individualistic culture centered on personal needs and desires, what are the strategies, or tactics, we could collectively mobilize to aspire to a political model of swarming that requires a degree of human collaboration that is sometimes instinctively present among certain animal species—the paradigmatic example of the swarm in your chapter comes not from fish and the currents they swim in, but from honeybees and the flowers they pollinate.

Let's change environment then and confront the following objection: some might say that *Homo sapiens* in the age of neoliberal capitalism seems often—not only, but often—restricted to playing the role of an individual, self-concerned, egotistic, and competitive consumer subject concerned with his/her individual needs, desires, and success. You, on the other hand, stress the need to actively and consciously promote collaborative swarm behavior to collectively counter the multiple human and nonhuman threats we're up against as new fascist movements pull us deeper in the age of the Anthropocene. How should we negotiate this contradictory push-pull?

BC: In that book, which came out in February 2017, there are preliminary reflections about Fascist danger, but the focus is elsewhere. The focus is on how large planetary processes like species evolution, the ocean conveyor system, glacier flows, and climate change intersect with each other and generate self-amplifying powers of their own. Earth scientists have recently—between the 1980s and the 1990s—broken previous assumptions about planetary gradualism that earlier earth scientists such as the geologist Charles Lyell and Charles Darwin made with such authority. There have been several punctuations of rapid, deep change in the past well before the Anthropocene; now there is another rapid change created by capitalism, replete with a series of planetary amplifiers. Planetary gradualism has bitten the dust, but a lot of humanists and human scientists, even those who worry about the Anthropocene, have not yet heard the news. *Haven't you heard? Gradualism is dead.* That affects everything.

When you see how the uneven effects of emissions from capitalist states team up with other planetary amplifiers with degrees of autonomy of their own, the question becomes how to generate a cross-regional pluralist assemblage of constituencies who come to terms with the Anthropocene and press regions, states, churches, universities, corporations, consumers, investment firms, and retirement funds to make radical changes over a short period of time. You must move on multiple fronts to both tame and redirect capitalist growth, as you look forward to a time when the perverse growth machine is brought under more severe control. So, what I mean by the "politics of swarming" does speak to the kinds of things we were just discussing.

The politics of swarming moves on multiple scales, going back and forth to amplify each in relation to the others. One register involves experimenting with role assignments that we pursue in daily life. It's related to what Foucault meant by the "specific intellectual," but is now extended to what might be called "specific citizens." If, say, you are relatively well-off in a high-emitting regime, you change the kind of car you drive, the occasions you ride a bike, the ways you press a neighborhood association to take action with respect to ecological issues, the way in which—if you are a teacher, as we both are—you change your courses to highlight these issues, and so forth. You alter a series of role definitions, connecting to people and institutions in new ways. Some collective effects are generated here. But, the key point is how creative role experiments work on the visceral registers of cultural pre-understandings, perception, judgment, and relationality. They move them. They thus prepare us to take new actions in other domains. We, in effect, work tactically upon our relational selves to open them to new contacts and to insulate them from Trumpian rhetoric.

Now other scales of politics can be engaged in a new key: protests, boycotts, electoral politics, creating eco-sanctuaries, copying tactics that have worked in other regions. As the activities escalate and as we encounter new events—a rapidly escalating glacier melt, a new upsurge of climate refugees, vigilante actions against climate activists, etc.—it may now be possible to forge a cross-regional assemblage, applying new pressure from the inside and outside upon states, corporations, churches, universities, temples, neighborhoods, and elected officials to take radical action. A politics of swarming acts at many sites at once.

These cross-regional assemblages may not be *that* likely to emerge, of course. But in the contemporary condition it becomes a piece of crackpot realism to say, "OK, let's forget it then." For the urgency of time makes it essential to probe actions that may be possible in relation to *needs* of the day. The politics of swarming *could* perhaps crystallize into cross-regional general strikes, as constituencies inspire each other into peaceful and urgent modes of action. A cross-regional strike is what I call an "improbable necessity" because the situation is more stark than those imagine who have ignored the history of planetary volatility before the advent of the Anthropocene. They overlook how planetary gradualism was never true and is not true now; hence they miss the autonomous role volatile planetary forces play *now* as CO_2 emissions trigger amplifiers that generate results greatly exceeding the force of the triggers.

By "swarming" I mean action on multiple fronts across several constituencies and regions that speak to the urgency and scope of the issues we face. Since we have seen several times in the past how capitalism can be stretched and turned in new directions, as well as how imbricated it is with a series of forces that exceed it, the interim task is to stretch it now and then to see how to tame further the growth imperatives it secretes.

NL: *Facing the Planetary* starts with a myth, and although the book itself is not about fascism but about self-regulating planetary processes, the question of myth is also relevant to our discussion for it is genealogically related to fascism. Myth was, in fact, appropriated by fascists and Nazis alike to promote a racist, anti-Semitic ideology.

I'm thinking in particular of Alfred Rosenberg's *The Myth of the 20th Century*, which was not as influential as Hitler's *Mein Kampf*, but was nonetheless one of the bestsellers of the Third Reich. Addressing a distressed, disappointed, and suffering population in the aftermath of the Great War going through a severe economic crisis, Rosenberg articulated the ideology of Nazism by promoting the Aryan racial myth and the necessary to root the German *Volk* back in an essentialist and nationalist conception of "blood and soil."

Much of what we've just said about rhetoric equally applies to the power of myth to move the masses on a visceral/mimetic register, and precisely for this reason, political theorists, starting very early, actually all the way back to Plato, have tended to be critical of myth and set out to oppose, or even exclude, the mythic, along with the affective registers it mediates.

Interestingly, however, even Plato—in his dramatization of the ideal republic—cannot avoid the mythic. In his critique of Homer or Hesiod, in the early books of *Republic* and in other dialogues as well, he relies on mythic elements, such as characters, dialogues, allegories, gods, heroes, and so forth. Somewhere in *Laws* he even says that this ideal polity has been constructed as a "dramatization of a noble and perfect lie," or myth. There is thus a sense in which Plato opposes myth via myth, or relies on a philosophical register that includes the mythic to discredit mythic fictions as lies far removed from the truth. He is thus relevant for our discussion.

Of course, you work within a very different, actually opposed, political ontology, one based on becoming over Being, immanence rather than transcendence, horizontality much more than verticality. Still, one could detect a similar strategic move in your appropriation of myth from the *Book of Job* that prefaces *Facing the Planetary*, in the sense that you

counter-myth of ascending to a transcendent level at which you gain an intuitive grasp of the Forms—it's an intuitive grasp. He knows that he can't simply prove such an ascension, then; rather, he produces a myth to support the possibility. But his myth is different from some he opposes because it arises out of a dialogue in which characters pose questions about it, continue to have doubts about it, and so on. Aristophanes is never convinced. So, it's not just one myth vs. another; this mythic mode is sprinkled with reflective dimensions—and that's true of Nietzsche as well.

You take Alfred Rosenberg, whom you know better than I do. I will take Hitler. Hitler also focuses on the centrality of a racial myth. He saw one day, according to his testimony in *Mein Kampf*, how Jews provided the "red thread" tying everything he hated together: he could tie them to social democracy, to communism, to miscegenation, to shopkeepers, and to other things he wanted to oppose. He presents the racial myth of the Aryan people as an authoritative myth that must be accepted; he terrorized everyone on the other side of it: Jews, homosexuals, Romani, social democrats, and others who resisted its "truth." Today he would call its opponents purveyors of Fake News.

When I present in the preface of *Facing the Planetary* a discussion of the *Book of Job* as a myth, I draw upon the testimonial in the Theophany in which the Nameless One speaks to Job out of a whirlwind or tornado. Job thus allows us to see and feel how our dominant spiritual traditions include some characterizations of planetary processes and nonhuman beings that are neither oriented to human mastery nor expressive of a world organically predisposed to us. Neither-nor. The world is worthy of embrace despite that, in part because it enables us to be. The new work in the earth sciences on planetary processes encourages us to think anew with and through such an orientation, to respect a planet with periodic volatilities, replete with multiple trajectories that intersect and exceed our capacities to master; a planet that will not even become that smooth and slow if we start now to tread lightly upon it.

There are strong premonitions of such an image in the *Book of Job*. You can hear them also elsewhere, as Bruno Latour has shown with his reading of Gaia, the volatile image of the planet developed from Hesiod. And so, we can sometimes engage myths to jostle dangerous assumptions and demands settled into the background of our thinking, practices, theories, and activities, opening them up for new reflection. Because there is never a vacuum on the visceral register of cultural life; there are always background premonitions that in-form life. They need to be jostled on occasion. The Anthropocene is a new era, but the rapid shifts it portends are not unique. It is only recently that capitalism has become the key catalyzing agent of planetary change—in dynamic relation to other volatile forces.

Nietzsche was right to say that myth, as a condensation of cultural preunderstandings and insistences, works on the visceral register of being in its modes of presentation, its rhythms of expression, and so forth. I agree with you that we are never in a world in which there is not some kind of mythic background sliding into preunderstandings, modes of perception, and prejudgments. The mythic is not to be eliminated; it is, rather, to be approached much differently than Hitler or Rosenberg approached it, along at least two dimensions: you resist and challenge the myth of the racial

Volk, challenging *both* its falsity and the visceral hatreds that fuel support for it; you then jostle the reassuring myth of planetary gradualism with counter-understandings of planetary processes.

I do not want to eliminate the mythic, and I'm guessing that Plato, whom you have studied more deeply, did not want to either. You could also take an early-modern thinker such as Hobbes who tells you to get rid of rhetorical figures and mythic arguments. Then you read Hobbes carefully and realize he is a rhetorical genius and knows himself to be one. The mythic never disappears: you can draw upon it to disturb and shake cultural predispositions about the planet that continue to hover in the background of the thinking, spirituality, and demands of so many people in old capitalist states. At least the *Book of Job* helps to loosen up undergrads in my classes as they encounter again a childhood story they thought they had already engaged. That's the way I'm trying to think about it.

NL: Your interest in the mythic and the way it operates on what you call the visceral register resonates very much with what I was saying about the mimetic dimension of human beings, or *Homo mimeticus*. I should add that despite the emphasis on representation, in recent years there has been a revival of attention in the fundamental biological, psychological, anthropological, and, since the discovery of mirror neurons, neurological fact that we are, nolens volens, imitative animals that respond—emotionally, affectively, and often unconsciously—to the myths we are told, including, of course, political myths.

A new picture of myths relevant to fascist politics thus emerges: myths are not simply false imitations of reality we can see from a safe distance. Rather, myths have a destabilizing formative and transformative power—Nietzsche also calls it a *pathos*—that spills over the walls of representation to affect and infect, by affective contagion, our psychic and political lives as well. Myth as a lie can easily turn into myth as a way of life.

BC: I would be interested to hear a bit more concerning your own thinking about the role of myth. Is myth, to you, both indispensable and dangerous? Do we need myth to combat the dangers of myth, and other tactics as well? If myth is ambiguous, what makes it so for beings such as it is?

NL: I agree with you that myth can't be eliminated. The ambivalence of mimesis and the one of myth are actually entangled in interesting ways. When I first read the *Republic*, I remember being struck by the way myth and mimesis, for Plato, are really two faces of the same coin. His strategy of attack is also similar: just as Plato critiques mimesis via the mimetic genre of the dialogue, so he attacks myth via a philosophical logos that continues to rely on myth. This is perhaps why Nietzsche mischievously says that Plato invented a new literary genre, namely, the novel. I like to think it's a Socratic irony he inherits from Plato.

So, yes, myth is both dangerous and indispensable. Myth is traditionally linked to lies, war, and violence, and in this first sense it is part of the danger we are facing today, not the solution. This is also Plato's position with respect to the mythmakers of his day: poets, rhapsodes, and sophists. The stories they spin represent realities that are not true, for they do not fit his ideal vision of rational Forms; they are not based on dialectical arguments but on divine inspirations. He linked them to lies, shadows, and phantoms instead. If we take this definition of myth, we notice that the media have changed but the shadows continue to surround us. They are so pervasive in our media environment that they have been blurring the very distinction between truth and lies, material facts and so called alternative facts, inaugurating the age of post-truth. I guess Plato would have seen this state of affairs as the total victory of myth over philosophy! We remain, more than ever, chained in caves, magnetized by shadows of our own making.

If the Platonic lesson that we are mimetic creatures is true, and I think it is, the mythmaker always has a certain advantage over the philosopher, for myths speak to people's mimetic faculties. And yet, as you have also stressed, this does not mean that myth, just like mimesis, cannot be resisted, reframed, and retold, perhaps using the very tools of myth—not to escape from the cave into an ideal world, but to create alternative immanent worlds. This second move seems to me intimately connected to a less visible, but not less fundamental dimension of myth that concerns its power of affection, formation, and transformation.

Stories have a formative power, and if we hear them in childhood, they will remain constitutive of who we are. Once again this is both good and bad news. Myth generates a feeling of belonging, unity, and transcendental reassurance that ties us to a destiny bigger than ours—often the destiny of a community, a nation, a chosen people protected by a tribal God. To a certain degree, this need for a narrative to give national unity to a people is understandable. It speaks to deeply-seated human needs to belong to an identity larger than oneself and remains necessary to provide a certain stability to one's worldview. However, such national myths often trigger the ethnocentric feeling that our nation is greater than the others, our God a better god, that our people are chosen people, and so on.

This territorial side of myth was of course powerfully exploited by fascist and Nazi regimes. I mentioned Rosenberg's *The Myth of the 20th Century*, which is not a popular book, so I was surprised that it had sold more than a million copies by 1945. It relies on the same anti-Semitic, racist ideology central to *Mein Kampf*. Rosenberg also adds an emphasis on Nordic mythology, which he considers necessary to set up a difference between racial types. The German *Volk*, he says, was the product of a certain "blood and soil," *Blut und Boden*, and so it's rooted in *nature*.

But in a contradiction that doesn't trouble the myth-maker, he also adds that so-called superior races need to be rooted in an Aryan mythology, and thus in a specific *culture*. It's as if Rosenberg sensed that blood alone is not sufficient to create national unity. Since blood purity is a fiction, all fascist ideologues need myths too to give form to a people. The horrors generated in the name of this myth in Germany were unprecedented, but unfortunately there is nothing exceptional in these hypernationalist, ethnocentric, and racist feelings. To different degrees, we find them in all nations; they are particularly appealing in times of loss of national identity and economic crisis—for innocent victims can be blamed for the failure of mythic dreams. If these fascist tendencies are easy to denounce in theory (especially in other nations), their affective power is more difficult to acknowledge, let alone eradicate in practice (especially in our nation).

That said, there are good and bad fictions, and so myths can have the very opposite effect as well. They have the affective power to open up new worlds, generate encounters with different cultures, trigger the desire to travel to other territories rather than protect one's own territory.

Since myth operates on a personal level, let me briefly switch to a confessional mode. I remember discovering early on in my life the power of myth via a PBS interview between Bill Moyers and the mythologist Joseph Campbell in the 1990s. It was titled *The Power of Myth* (as I say in the introduction, childhood impressions can be lasting). I was a teenager growing up in a remote village in the Italian-speaking side of the Alps and I was captivated by this American scholar of myth who was also a brilliant storyteller. His motif was the one of the hero's journey and the process of maturation that ensues from crossing a threshold and entering a different world where tests and trials need to be confronted for maturation to ensue. Viewers of *Star Wars*, or any other adventure, should be familiar with the journey.

Campbell's archetypal approach to myth might be a bit outdated today, but his lesson that myths should not be taken literally but interpreted for their symbolic potential, educative power, and spiritual insights that belong to

Closer to us, I also found strikingly contemporary values in founding short stories like Washington Irving's "Rip Van Winkle," for instance, which promotes the importance of adventure, the rediscovery of our mythic past, and the centrality of storytelling in providing a sense of direction during periods of historical transition in a culture perhaps excessively concerned with material values; or in Lewis Carroll's *Alice in Wonderland*, an adventure book that, not unlike myth, celebrates a world of playful transformation over one of stability; or, my children's favorite right now, Homer's *Odyssey*, a founding myth that illustrates not one but many figures, and is thus not ideal in Plato's sense. If it's at times problematic in its assumptions, especially with respect to gender, it also stresses the importance of resilience, hospitality, and the immanent vitality of diplomatic speeches over mere violence in order to survive a perilous journey back home—wherever home may be.

My sense, then, is that all these different myths and many others that have withstood the test of time are part of a legacy we can draw from, as parents, teachers, and citizens. They have something to teach future generations confronted with mythic distinctions between good and evil, us and them. If these oppositions play in favor of new fascist leaders, they no longer hold in a world of transformation characteristic of the Anthropocene. And since transformation, encounters, and processes of becoming that involve human and nonhuman others have been central components of myth from time immemorial, I also like to think that dominant territorial myths can be countered by alternative mythic traditions. Anyway, as long as my children enjoy the stories, I'll keep reading.

Tyranny, Strikes, Resistance

NL: We have been joining forces in the past years to confront challenging shadows on the horizon. To establish another genealogical bridge with other thinkers who are currently countering the rise of new fascist movements, I would like you to comment on a recent book that, in many ways, resonates with our discussion: Timothy Snyder's *On Tyranny: Twenty Lessons from the Twentieth Century* (2017). In this little but illuminating book, Snyder, who is an American historian specialized in the history of the Holocaust, shares the presupposition with which we started: namely, that it's necessary to learn from the strategies mobilized by fascist and Nazi leaders and ideologues in the 1930s and '40s in order to steer contemporary constituencies away from the political reenactment of those horrifying possibilities.

To that end, Snyder offers a series of practical, action-oriented suggestions that structure the book and help us counter the rise of fascism, suggestions like "Do Not Obey in Advance," or "Defend Institutions," or "Believe in Truth." He offers twenty of them, but I would like to zoom in on Lesson 8, titled "Stand Out," for it seems in line with a principle necessary to develop what you call "politics of swarming" and counters forces that I call "mimetic crowds." In favor of standing out from the crowd, Snyder writes: "Someone has to. It is easy to follow along. It can feel strange to do or say something different. But without that unease, there is no freedom. Remember Rosa Parks. The moment you set an example, the spell of the status quo is broken and others will follow." There is a double movement at play in this passage not obey in advance," that is, resist tacitly going along to get along. I think of that as congruent with the themes of role experimentations mentioned earlier. Role experiments create room within the things that you regularly do, like work, raising kids, attending church, relating to neighbors, writing, retirement investments, teaching, etc. You then take a step here, a step there, outside settled expectations, because there is often room to do things that exceed merely going along to get along. They make a difference in a cumulative effect, yes. But the most important effect is the way they help to recode our tacit presumptions and orientations to collective action. Even small things.

In this spirit, I recently used Facebook to write an open letter to Donald Trump after he withdrew from the Paris Accord. Making such a minor public statement can coalesce with innumerable others doing similar things. People shared it; it received a broader hearing; even some trolls ridiculed it. It would not be easy to take back. The accumulation of such minor actions counters the scary drive to allow Trumpism to become normalized. Charles Blow, the *New York Times* columnist, also keeps us focused on that issue.

I like several things about Snyder's book, but I think—maybe I am wrong, for I might not have read it carefully enough—that it is kind of limited to what you and I, as individuals and small groups, can do. Today we need to join these small acts to the larger politics of swarming, out of which new cross-regional citizen assemblages grow. Such assemblages themselves, in the ways they coalesce and operate horizontally, expose fallacies in the Fascist leadership principle. Protests at town meetings, for instance, fit Snyder's theme, I am sure.

But let's suppose, as could well happen, that the Antarctic glacier starts melting at such a rapid rate we see how its consequences are going to be extremely severe over a short period of time. (The computer models are usually three to five years behind what actually happens on the ice, ground, and atmosphere.) Constituencies in several regions could now mobilize around this event to organize general strikes, putting pressure on states and corporations from inside and outside at the same time. So, the main way I would supplement Snyder is to explore the horizontal mobilization of larger assemblages, to speak to the urgency of time during a period when dominant states so far resist doing enough.

Further, from my point of view, electoral politics poses severe problems; but there is also a dilemma of electoral politics that must be engaged honestly. Electoral victories can be stymied by many forces. But you must not use that fact as a reason to desist. For, as some of us have argued on the blog *The Contemporary Condition* for several years, if and when the right wing gains control of all branches of government, you run the severe risk of a Fascist takeover. So, participate in elections and act on other fronts as well. Indeed, in the United States the evangelical/capitalist resonance machine has acted in its way on multiple fronts simultaneously for decades. The Right believes in its version of the politics of swarming.

The way to respond to the dilemma of electoral politics is to expand beyond it but not to eliminate it as one site of activity. For, again, if the right wing controls the courts, the presidency, both houses of Congress, the intelligence agencies, and a lot of state legislators, they can generate cumulative effects that will be very difficult to reverse.

Aspirational Fascists, for instance, use such victories to suppress minority voting. So, multiple modes and registers of politics. I wouldn't be surprised if Snyder and I agree on that.

NL: I think you're right. In Snyder's longer genealogy of fascism and Nazism, *Black Earth*, of which the little book is in many ways a distillation, he ends with a chapter titled "Our World," which situates fascist politics in the broader context of climate change and collective catastrophes along the lines you also suggested in *Facing the Planetary*. The more voices promoting pluralist assemblages contra the nihilism of fascist crowds, the better!

Anti-Fascism

NL: Speaking of little books, then, I hear you are yourself working on a new short book dealing with some of the issues we have been discussing, which is provisionally titled *Aspirational Fascism*. To conclude, and amplify anti-fascist diagnostics could you briefly delineate its general content, scope, and some of the main lessons you hope will be retained?

BC: This will be a short, quickly executed book, a pamphlet, that could come out within a year. It's divided into three chapters, and it will probably be around one hundred pages. The first chapter reviews similarities and differences between Hitler's rhetoric and crowd management and those of Donald Trump. It also attends to how the pluralizing Left has too often ignored the real grievances of the white working class, helping inadvertently to set it up for a Trump takeover. The second chapter explores how a set of severe bodily drills and disciplines in pre-Nazi Germany helped to create men particularly attuned to Hitler's rhetoric in the wake of the loss of World War I and the Great Depression. You and I are having this conversation today in Weimar, a sweet, lovely, artistic town. Hitler, I am told, gave over twenty speeches here, in the central *platz*, to assembled throngs.

So, in the second chapter I attend to how coarse rhetorical strategies, severe bodily practices, and extreme events work back and forth on each other. That chapter is indebted to a book by Klaus Theweleit, *Male Fantasies* (1987, 2 vols.); it helps me to attend to how specific bodily disciplines and drills attune people to particular rhetorical practices and insulate them from others. The themes Theweleit pursues are then carried into the United States of today as we explore how the neglect of real white working-class grievances, the military training and job disciplines many in that class face, and the interminable Trump campaign work back and forth upon one another. That is why I never understate the need to attend to our own bodily disciplines, habits, and role practices.

The third chapter is designed to show how what I call multifaceted pluralism is both good in itself and generates the best mode of resistance to Fascist movements. *Multifaceted* means that it supports generous, responsive modes of affective communications and bodily interrelations; it also means that the new pluralism treats the white working class as one of the minorities to nourish, even as we also oppose the ugly things a portion of it does. That support must first include folding egalitarian projects into those noble drives to pluralization that have been in play; it must also include taking radical action to respond to the Anthropocene before it generates so much ocean acidification, expansive drought, ocean rising, and increasing temperatures that the resulting wars and refugee pressures will provide even more happy hunting grounds for aspirational Fascism.

The pluralizing Left must come to terms immediately with the need to ameliorate class inequality in job conditions, retirement security, and workplace authority. That deserves as much attention as the politics of pluralization itself. I pursue a model of egalitarian pluralism, then, that challenges both liberal individualism and the image of a smooth communist future, seeing both to be insufficient to counter the twin dangers of Fascism and the Anthropocene today. There are no smooth ideals to pursue on this rocky planet. But there may be ways to enhance our attachment to a planet that exceeds the contending adventures of mastery that dominated the nineteenth and twentieth centuries.

Those are the three parts of the book. I realize, for sure, that the project makes for heavy lifting, that it will be difficult to convince some pluralists to push an egalitarian agenda and some segments of the working class to take the

Anthropocene seriously. But the two projects are interrelated and imperative, and it is possible that advances on the first front could loosen more people up to accept action on the second.

Against the dangers of Fascism, I do not project either a communitarian ideal or a single-minded liberalism concentrated on the reflective register of public deliberation. A multifaceted democracy combines together a diversity of voices, a broad spectrum ethos that speaks on several registers of cultural life, economic egalitarianism, a periodic politics to bring new diversities into being, and a readiness by those who appreciate a multifaceted culture to create a militant pluralist assemblage from time to time to fight against aspirational Fascism when it raises its ugly head. I think that you have participated in a tradition in which the search for community is matched by the disavowal of its closure. Could you say more about your current thinking on this matter? It seems to be a timely question today.

NL: Yes, I share this pluralist view and I'm equally skeptical of communitarian ideals for the mimetic reasons we discussed in relation to both myth and mimesis. The formation of a community runs the risk of relying on myths that promote a type of nationalist, organic, and tribal closure we have witnessed in the 1920s and 1930s and is currently reemerging in the present period, both in Europe and in the United States. In a sense, while I'm far from opposed to elective communities of few individuals in practice, it's precisely this skepticism concerning the theoretical origins of fin de siècle discourses of community that encouraged me to return to this concept from a genealogical perspective that is haunted by the phantom of fascist communities.

The link between mimesis and community was present in figures like Sigmund Freud, for instance, who posited the problematic of identification at the heart of a mythic founding murder. You equally find it at work in René Girard, who establishes a connection between sacrifice, violence, and communal formations predicated on scapegoating mechanisms. If identification plays a role in the election of a new fascist leader, scapegoating continues to be at play today, especially against racial, gendered, and religious minorities. Even earlier, you find the concept of community at work in sociologists like Ferdinand Tönnies, who set up an opposition between a mechanical, atomistic modern society (or *Gesellschaft*) and a pre-industrial conception of an organic community (or *Gemeinschaft*).

But as your question suggests, this is not what most scholars have primarily in mind when they speak of community these days. Starting in the 1980s and 1990s, the focus has progressively shifted from organic communities that advocated mimetic closure to inoperative communities predicated on heterogeneous plurality. Figures like Jean-Luc Nancy and Maurice Blanchot, for instance, have been pivotal in generating a renewal of interest in this old concept in order to rethink the ontological foundations of politics beyond the horizon of the two dominant paradigms of community in the twentieth century: namely, communism and fascism. A deconstruction of community launched this concept on the theoretical scene, and especially in literary theory and continental philosophy, it's still a hot topic.

My approach is inscribed in both these modern and postmodern traditions. But rather than stressing the inoperative quality of community, I'm more concerned with the danger of communal movements that might become quite operative again. In an article [now chapter two of this volume] on community, I thus took a genealogical step back to a figure who is not often discussed by contemporary social theorists but who relied on a modern sociological tradition attentive to violent communal movements and, at the same time, provided both Nancy and Blanchot with a theoretical starting point to reframe this concept: namely, Georges Bataille.

I found it important to go back to Bataille's writings of the 1930s because as he first started thinking about community, he explicitly did so in the context of the rise of fascist movements. It also seemed crucial to stress that the Bataillean concept of community cannot be peeled off from what he called "the psychological structure of fascism" in order to call attention to the fact that community is a concept that is fundamentally ambivalent and can thus be put to both fascist and revolutionary use. Nancy is fully aware of this ambivalence. But more recent theorists have paid less attention to the genealogical affiliation between community and fascism.

The positive aura that surrounds postmodern accounts of linguistic communities led me to focus on its darker affective and historical side. My main goal was thus not to promote community as a concept that should necessarily be recuperated politically today. Bataille was nonetheless particularly useful for diagnosing the heterogeneous movements of "attraction and repulsion" that fascist leaders who are "totally other" can generate in the crowd of followers. He provided a historical and theoretical framework to think critically about the contemporary resurgence of new fascist leaders who are currently channeling affective forces we still need to come to terms with. Looking back to the rise of European fascism seemed a way to begin to recognize that if not fascism itself, the mimetic drive toward a new form of fascism I tried to outline might still be secretly at play in rising communal movements. I grouped them under the rubric of the "mimetic community" to call attention to the danger of fusional sameness.

That said, I also find that, at the micro-level, Bataille's concept of "elective community" resonates with your definition of a pluralist assemblage or swarm that is open to heterogeneous connections. There might be productive, inclusive, and nonviolent modes of resistance to fascism in joining these traditions, since positive, life-affirmative forms of mimesis are central to both. The ambivalence we spoke of in relation to myth and mimesis might be equally operative in relation to community. This is also true in practice. Once people assemble, it's always difficult to predict what the outcome will be. As Bataille, echoing Durkheim, used to say, there is a force in the group that is more than the sum of its parts. Violence and the erasure of differences is always a danger, as Girard and Bataille remind us. Still, there is also an opportunity for nonviolent resistance to fascism in pluralist assemblages, as you and Judith Butler invite us to consider. In any case, the Janus-faced properties of mimesis always lead me to try to look both ways, which, I like to think, is another heterogeneous connection between our anti-fascist perspectives.

To conclude on an affirmative note, let me stress the importance of the general strike that you call an "improbable necessity." In the wake of the cumulative scandalous political actions and mimetic reactions that do not simply

Notes

Preface

1. Friedrich Nietzsche, *Daybreak*, trans. R. J. Hollingdale (Cambridge: Cambridge University Press, 1982), 61.

2. For a more detailed account of the role mimesis plays in the crowd behavior of European fascism, see Nidesh Lawtoo, *The Phantom of the Ego: Modernism and the Mimetic Unconscious* (East Lansing: Michigan State University Press, 2013), 68–83, 130–62, 181–208, 209–33, 247–80. On the similarities and differences between my take on "mimetic pathos" and Girard's theory of "mimetic desire," see *Phantom*, 4–6, 281–305.

3. Umberto Eco, "Ur-Fascism," *New York Review of Books*, June 22, 1995.

Introduction

1. Friedrich Nietzsche, *The Gay Science*, trans. Walter Kaufmann (New York: Vintage Books, 1974), 303.

2. On the mimetic unconscious, see Nidesh Lawtoo, *The Phantom of the Ego: Modernism and the Mimetic Unconscious* (East Lansing: Michigan State University Press, 2013), 13–19; "The Mimetic Unconscious: A Genealogy," in *Imitation, Contagion, Suggestion: Rethinking the Social*, ed. Christian Borch (New York: Routledge, 2019), 37–53.

3. Timothy Snyder, *The Road to Unfreedom: Russia, Europe, America* (London: Penguin, 2018). Unfortunately, this groundbreaking book appeared too late to be fully integrated here. It reveals disconcerting new evidence of Russia's implication in the 2016 U.S. presidential election, unmasking Donald Trump as "an American loser who became a Russian tool" (219; see also 217–76). Interestingly, Snyder steps back to the fascist philosopher Ivan Ilyin in order to trace his influence on Russia's current development of a "politics of eternity" that transcends historical facts in order to promote myths of greatness via a logic of the

spectacle that is now center stage in U.S. politics as well. In the process, he offers an informed historical account of "the fascism of the Russian assault upon the European Union and the United States, of which the Trump campaign is a part" (215). I note that as a historian, Snyder's focus on how fascist "ideas from the past can matter in the present" (16) and his awareness that the Internet plays a key role in the "invisible manipulation of personalities" (224) is in line with what I call, echoing Nietzsche, genealogy, and with the tradition of the mimetic unconscious genealogy uncovers.

4. For a representative sample of recent works that calls attention to the rising threat of fascism, see Timothy Snyder, *On Tyranny: Twenty Lessons from the Twentieth Century* (New York: Tim Duggan Books, 2017); Noam Chomsky, *Requiem for the American Dream: The 10 Principles of Concentration of Wealth and Power* (New York: Seven Stories Press, 2017); William E. Connolly, *Aspirational Fascism: The Struggle for Multifaceted Democracy under Trumpism* (Minneapolis: University of Minnesota Press, 2017); Madeleine Albright, *Fascism: A*

Warning (New York: HarperCollins, 2018); and Jason Stanley, *How Fascism Works: The Politics of Us and Them* (New York: Random House, 2018). See also the special issues of *Theory and Event* 20, no. 1 (2017), *L'Esprit Créateur* 57, no. 4 (2017), and *MLN* 132, no. 5 (2017), where I first approached the question of (new) fascism.

5. Umberto Eco, "Ur-Fascism," *New York Review of Books*, June 22, 1995.

6. Timothy Snyder, *Black Earth: The Holocaust as History and Warning* (London: Bodley Head, 2015), 320.

7. As Snyder puts it: "Fascism begins not with an assessment of what is within, but from a rejection of what is without." Snyder, *Road to Unfreedom*, 26.

8. For a psycho-sociological account of the authoritarian personality among the general population in terms of submission, toughness, aggression, anti-intellectualism, excessive sexuality, and the like, see Theodor W. Adorno et al., *The Authoritarian Personality* (New York: Harper and Brothers, 1950), 248–50.

9. As Arendt puts it: "This impermanence no doubt has something to do with the proverbial fickleness of the

masses and the fame that rests on them; more likely, it can be traced to the perpetual-motion mania of totalitarian movements which can remain in power only so long as they keep moving and set everything around them in motion." Hannah Arendt, *The Origins of Totalitarianism* (New York: A Harvest Book, 1976), 306.

10. I first introduced the logic of mimetic patho(-)logy this study furthers in *Phantom*, 6–8.

11. Friedrich Nietzsche, *On the Genealogy of Morals*, trans. Douglas Smith (Oxford: Oxford University Press, 1998), 3.

12. Ibid., 3, 13.

13. Ibid., 43.

14. Nietzsche adds that genealogy requires "some schooling in history and philology, together with an innate sense of discrimination with respect to questions of psychology"; ibid., 5. What follows furthers this perspectival method to dissect the power of fascist *pathos*.

15. On hypermimesis, see Lawtoo, *Conrad's Shadow: Catastrophe, Mimesis, Theory* (East Lansing: Michigan State University Press, 2016), 293–330; Lawtoo, "The *Matrix* E-Motion: Simulation, Mimesis, Hypermimesis,"

in *Mimesis, Movies and Media: Violence, Desire, and the Sacred*, ed. Scott Cowdell, Chris Fleming, and Joel Hodge (London: Bloomsbury, 2015), 89–104.

16. Snyder, *On Tyranny*, 61, 124.

17. Connolly, *Aspirational Fascism*, 6. As it will become clear in what follows, I am both indebted and grateful to Bill Connolly for numerous conversations, stimulating exchanges, and collaborative projects that inform the study at hand. While we approach fascism from different perspectives, our genealogies emerged from a dialogic encounter in which each perspective both echoes and supplements the other in a shared (Nietzschean) spirit that affirms a pluralist politics of friendship.

18. Robert O. Paxton, *The Anatomy of Fascism* (New York: Alfred A. Knopf, 2004), 14. On the "intrinsic flaws" of the "definitional approach," see also Kevin Passmore, *Fascism: A Very Short Introduction* (Oxford: Oxford University Press, 2002), 4–21. For informed historical studies of fascism, see also Roger Griffin and Matthew Feldman, eds., *Fascism: Critical Concepts in Political Science*, vol. 3. (London: Routledge, 2004); Roger Griffin,

ed., *International Fascism: Theory, Causes and the New Consensus* (London: Arnold, 1998); and George L. Mosse, *The Fascist Revolution: Towards a General Theory of Fascism* (New York: Howard Fertig, 1999).

19. Paxton, *The Anatomy of Fascism*, 4.

20. Giovanni Gentile and Benito Mussolini, *La dottrina del fascismo* (1932), http://www.polyarchy.org/basta/documenti/fascismo.1932.html (my translation).

21. Passmore, *Fascism*, 21.

22. Ibid., 2.

23. Gentile and Mussolini, *La dottrina*.

24. Ibid.

25. René Girard, *Des choses cachées depuis la fondation du monde* (Paris: Editions Grasset, 1978), 455.

26. Philippe Lacoue-Labarthe, *L'Imitation des modernes (Typographies II)* (Paris: Galilée, 1986), 282.

27. Regular members of the reading group included Jane Bennett, Anand Pandian, Naveeda Khan, and Emily Parker. I am grateful to all of them for the inspiring conversations we have had.

28. William Connolly, "Donald Trump and the New Fascism,"

http://contemporarycondition.blogspot.de/2016/08/
donald-trump-and-new-fascism.html; and Connolly,
"Trump, Putin and the Big Lie Scenario," http://
contemporarycondition.blogspot.de/2017/01/trump-
putin-and-big-lie-scenario.html.

29. Participants included Paola Marrati, Ann Smock, Rochelle
Tobias, Christopher Fynsk, Jane Bennett, Jean-Luc Nancy,
Hent de Vries, and Avital Ronell. The proceedings of the
conference were published in a special issue of *MLN* titled
"Poetics and Politics: With Lacoue-Labarthe," ed. Nidesh
Lawtoo, *MLN* 132, no. 5 (2017).

30. For more information about the project, see http://www.
homomimeticus.eu/.

31. Having included a draft of chapter 2 in his syllabus for his
seminar on fascism, Connolly kindly invited me to offer
a presentation in his seminar at Johns Hopkins in the
spring of 2017; I reciprocated the gesture by inviting him
to present a section of his book *Aspirational Fascism* on
a panel I chaired at MLA titled "The Rhetoric of (New)
Fascism" in January 2018. Our collaboration is ongoing.

Chapter 1. Crowd Psychology Redux

1. On our violent origins, see René Girard, *Violence and the Sacred*, trans. Patrick Gregory (Baltimore: Johns Hopkins University Press, 1977). On our violent destination, see René Girard, *Battling to the End*, trans. Mary Baker (East Lansing: Michigan State University Press), 2010.

2. Jean-Pierre Dupuy, *La panique* (Paris: Seuil, 2003), 60 (my translation).

3. Ibid., 35. On mimetic theory and crowd psychology, see also Jean-Pierre Dupuy, *Dans l'oeil du cyclone: Colloque de Cerisy* (Paris: Carnet Nord, 2008); Paul Dumouchel, "Massengewalt und konstitutive Gewalt," in *Gewaltmassen: Ueber Eigendynamik und Selbstorganisation kollektiver Gewalt*, ed. Axel T. Paul and Benjamin Schwalb (Hamburg: Hamburger Edition, 2015), 103–23. For pioneering studies of mimesis and crowd behavior, see Mikkel Borch-Jacobsen, *The Freudian Subject*, trans. Catherine Porter (Stanford, CA: Stanford University Press, 1988); Philippe Lacoue-Labarthe and Jean-Luc Nancy, "La panique politique," in *Retreating the Political*, ed. Simon Sparks (New York: Routledge, 1977), 1–28. I'll return to Borch-Jacobsen,

Lacoue-Labarthe, and Nancy below.

4. Robert O. Paxton, *The Anatomy of Fascism* (New York: Alfred A. Knopf, 2004), 40, 41.

5. Ibid., 219.

6. For a more detailed account of Nietzsche's critique of fascism, which is implicated in the mimetic forces it denounces, see Nidesh Lawtoo, *The Phantom of the Ego: Modernism and the Mimetic Unconscious* (East Lansing: Michigan State University Press, 2013), esp. 68–83.

7. Gustave Le Bon, *Psychologie des foules* (Paris: Presses Universitaires de France, 1963), 13, 74 (my translation).

8. Gabriel Tarde, *Les lois de l'imitation* (Paris: Seuil, 2001), 97, 50 (my translation).

9. Girard, *Violence and the Sacred*, 76, 79.

10. While Girard is not a reference in Serge Moscovici's informed account of crowd psychology, the latter nonetheless mentions "the mimetic desire in all of us to behave like someone else." Serge Moscovici, *The Age of the Crowd: A Historical Treatise on Mass Psychology*, trans. J. C. Whitehouse (Cambridge: Cambridge University Press, 1985), 161.

11. What follows is an extension of a genealogy that links crowd psychology (esp. Le Bon, Tarde, and Freud), mimetic contagion, and fascist politics, which has its foundations in Lawtoo, *Phantom of the Ego*, esp. 77–83, 226–80. For informed sociological accounts of crowd psychology, see also Moscovici, *The Age of the Crowd*; Christian Borch, *The Politics of Crowds: An Alternative History of Sociology* (Cambridge: Cambridge University Press, 2012); and Christian Borch, ed. *Imitation, Contagion, and Suggestion: On Mimesis and Society* (New York: Routledge, 2019).

12. Le Bon, *Psychologie des foules*, 14; my translation.

13. See Lawtoo, *Phantom of the Ego*, 109–10, 123.

14. See Geoff Shullenberger, "The Scapegoating Machine," *The New Inquiry*, November 30, 2016.

15. Le Bon, *Psychologie des foules*, 36.

16. Ibid., 26.

17. Ibid., 36.

18. Tarde, *Lois de l'imitation*, 128.

19. Ibid., 137.

20. And Canetti adds: "It is for the sake of this equality that

people become a crowd and they tend to overlook anything which might detract from it." Elias Canetti, *Crowds and Power*, trans. Carol Stewart (New York: Ferrar, Straus and Giroux, 1962), 29.

21. Hannah Arendt, *The Origins of Totalitarianism* (New York: A Harvest Book, 1976), 305 n. 1.

22. Ibid.

23. Edward Bernays, *Propaganda* (New York: Ig Publishing, 2005), 37.

24. Ibid., 111, 47.

25. Moscovici, *The Age of the Crowd*, 4.

26. Ibid., 13, 75.

27. Borch, *The Politics of Crowds*, 303.

28. Ibid., 301.

29. Sigmund Freud, *Group Psychology and the Analysis of the Ego*, trans. James Strachey (New York: W.W. Norton & Co., 1959), 21.

30. Lawtoo, *The Phantom of the Ego*, 233–60. See also Borch-Jacobsen, *The Freudian Subject*, esp. 127–239; and Mikkel Borch-Jacobsen, *The Emotional Tie: Psychoanalysis, Mimesis, and Affect*, trans. Douglas Brick (Stanford, CA:

Stanford University Press, 1992), 1–35.

31. Freud, *Group Psychology*, 21.

32. Ibid., 38.

33. Ibid., 23, 38, 39.

34. Ibid., 37.

35. Girard, *Violence and the Sacred*, 171.

36. Ibid., 170.

37. Borch-Jacobsen, *The Freudian Subject*, 208; see also 127–239.

38. Borch-Jacobsen, *The Emotional Tie*, 2.

39. Freud, *Group Psychology*, 21.

40. William E. Connolly, *Aspirational Fascism: The Struggle for Multifaceted Democracy under Trumpism* (Minneapolis: University of Minnesota Press, 2018), 37. On Connolly's critique of Freud's account of group psychology, see also 36–44.

41. Mikkel Borch-Jacobsen, "Freudian Politics," in *The Emotional Tie*, 1–35.

42. Freud, *Group Psychology*, 9.

43. Tarde, *Lois de l'imitation*, 148.

44. Giacomo Rizzolatti and Corrado Sinigaglia, *Mirrors in*

the Brain: How Our Minds Share Actions and Emotions, trans. Frances Anderson (Oxford: Oxford University Press, 2008).

45. Rizzolatti and Sinigaglia, *Mirrors in the Brain*, 125.

46. On embodied simulation, see also Vittorio Gallese, "The Two Sides of Mimesis: Mimetic Theory, Embodied Simulation, and Social Identification," in *Mimesis and Science: Empirical Research on Imitation and the Mimetic Theory of Culture and Religion*, ed. Scott Garrels (East Lansing: Michigan State University Press, 2011), 87–108.

47. As Moscovici reminds us, "Le Bon urges that the methods of the theater should be taken up in the world of politics, with the stage as a model of social relationships in dramatic form and a place where those relationships were observed." Moscovici, *The Age of the Crowd*, 89.

48. Le Bon, *Psychologie des foules*, 2; Gabriel Tarde, *L'opinion et la foule* (Paris: Félix Alcan Editeur, 1901), 11.

49. Tarde, *L'opinion et la foule*, 5, 6.

50. Ibid., 4, 3.

51. Ibid., 17.

52. Ibid., 10, 13, 11.

53. Sloterdijk qtd. in Borch, *Politics of Crowds*, 283. Peter Sloterdijk, *Die Verachtung der Massen: Versuch über Kulturkämpfe in der modernen Gesellschaft* (Frankfurt: Suhrkamp, 2000), 25.

54. Ibid., 283.

55. Jean Baudrillard, "The Masses: The Implosion of the Social in the Media," *New Literary History* 16, no. 3 (1985): 577–89, 580.

56. Jean Baudrillard, *In the Shadow of the Silent Majorities*, trans. Paul Foss et al. (Los Angeles: Semiotext(e), 2007), 49.

57. Ibid., 50.

58. Timothy Snyder, *On Tyranny: Twenty Lessons from the Twentieth Century* (New York: Tim Duggan Books, 2017), 124, 61, 75, 74.

59. Umberto Eco, "Ur-Fascism," *New York Review of Books*, June 22, 1995, no pagination.

60. I signal belatedly that Timothy Snyder also recently recognized the role of *The Apprentice* in Trump's victory. As he puts it: "Trump outshone Republican rivals at debates thanks to years of practice at playing a fictional character on

television." Snyder, *The Road to Unfreedom: Russia, Europe, America* (London: Penguin, 2018), 222. Snyder's account of "the fictional character 'Donald Trump, successful businessman'" as a "fiction rested on fiction rested on fiction" (221, 222) provides compelling historical evidence that supports my hypermimetic hypothesis concerning the power of hyperreal fictions to form mimetic, all too mimetic lives.

61. Girard, *Deceit, Desire and the Novel: Self and Other in Literary Structure*, trans. Yvonne Freccero (Baltimore: Johns Hopkins University Press, 1965), 8.

62. Girard, *Violence and the Sacred*, 79.

63. George Bataille, "Hegel, la mort, le sacrifice," in Œuvres *complètes*, vol. 12 (Paris: Gallimard, 1988), 349–69, 337.

64. Ibid., 12:337.

65. Ibid., 12:336.

66. Ibid., 12:337.

67. On the relation between catharsis, contagion, and violence, see Nidesh Lawtoo, "Violence and the Mimetic Unconscious, Part One: The Cathartic Hypothesis (Aristotle, Freud, Girard)," *Contagion* 25 (2018):

159–92; and Nidesh Lawtoo, "Violence and the Mimetic Unconscious, Part Two: The Contagious Hypothesis (Plato, Affect, Mirror Neurons)," *Contagion* 26 (2019).

Chapter 2. The Mimetic Community

1. See Benedict Anderson, *Imagined Communities: Reflections on the Origins and Spread of Nationalism* (London: Verso, 1983); Jean-Luc Nancy, *The Inoperative Community*, ed. Peter Connor, trans. Peter Connor et al. (Minneapolis: University of Minnesota Press, 1991); Maurice Blanchot, *La communauté inavouable* (Paris: Les Éditions de Minuit, 1983); Jean-Luc Nancy, *The Disavowed Community*, trans. Paul Armstrong (New York: Fordham University Press, 2016); J. Hillis Miller, *The Conflagration of Community: Fiction before and after Auschwitz* (Chicago: University of Chicago Press, 2011); Giorgio Agamben, *The Coming Community*, trans. M. Hardt (Minneapolis: University of Minnesota Press, 1993); Nidesh Lawtoo, "The Laughter of Community," in *The Phantom of the Ego: Modernism and the Mimetic Unconscious* (East Lansing: Michigan State University Press, 2013), 295–304; Jean-Luc Nancy, "The

Common Growl," in *The Common Growl: Toward a Poetics of Precarious Community*, ed. Thomas Claviez, trans. Steven Corcoran (New York: Fordham University Press, 2016), vii–ix.

2. Nancy, "The Common Growl," ix.

3. Friedrich Nietzsche, *Daybreak*, trans. R. J. Hollingdale (Cambridge: Cambridge University Press, 1982), 106.

4. Eduardo Cadava, Peter Connor, and Jean-Luc Nancy, eds., *Who Comes after the Subject?* (New York: Routledge, 1991).

5. Nancy, *Inoperative Community*, 12.

6. Nancy, "The Common Growl," ix.

7. Nancy, *The Disavowed Community*, viii.

8. René Girard, *Battling to the End*, trans. Mary Baker (East Lansing: Michigan State University Press, 2010), 18.

9. See Ferdinand Tönnies, *Community and Society*, ed. and trans. C. P. Loomis (New York: Dover Publications, 1963); Sigmund Freud, *Totem and Taboo*, trans. A. A. Brill (Harmondsworth, UK: Penguin, 1940); René Girard, *Violence and the Sacred*, trans. P. Gregory (Baltimore: Johns Hopkins University Press, 1977).

10. Nancy, *Inoperative Community*, 25.

11. Roland Barthes, "From Work to Text," in *Image, Music, Text*, ed. and trans. S. Heath (London: Fontana Press, 1977), 157.

12. Girard, *Violence and the Sacred*, 222.

13. Georges Bataille, *Erotism: Death and Sensuality*, trans. Mary Dalwood (San Francisco: City Lights Books, 1986), 13.

14. Ibid., 8.

15. Philippe Lacoue-Labarthe, "Typography," in *Typography: Mimesis, Philosophy, Politics*, ed. Christopher Fynsk (Cambridge, MA: Harvard University Press, 1989), 43–138, 106 n. 103.

16. Girard, *Violence and the Sacred*, 222. On Bataille and mimetic theory, see Lawtoo, *Phantom*, chap. 4.

17. Anthony D. Traylor, "Violence Has Its Reasons: Girard and Bataille," *Contagion* 21 (2014): 131–56, 131.

18. For exceptions, see A. J. Mitchell and J. K. Winfree, eds., *The Obsessions of Georges Bataille: Community and Communication* (Albany, NY: SUNY Press, 2009); see also Patrick Ffrench, *After Bataille: Sacrifice, Exposure, Community* (London: Legenda, 2007), 107–50.

19. Nancy, *Inoperative Community*, 16.

20. Ibid., 19.

21. Ibid., 26.

22. Jean-Luc Nancy, *Being Singular Plural*, trans. R. D. Richardson and A. E. O'Byrne (Stanford, CA: Stanford University Press, 2000).

23. Georges Bataille, "Collège socratique," vol. 6 in *Œuvres complètes*, 12 vols. (Paris: Gallimard, 1970–88), 279. Unless indicated otherwise, all translations of Bataille's are the author's.

24. Nancy, *Inoperative Community*, 15.

25. Ibid., xxxviii, 14.

26. Ibid., 15.

27. Ibid., 26.

28. René Girard, *Evolution and Conversion: Dialogues on the Origins of Culture*. With Pierpaolo Antonello and João de Castro Rocha (London: Continuum, 2007), 252.

29. Georges Bataille, *L'expérience intérieure* (Paris: Gallimard, 1954), 112.

30. Georges Bataille, "Lettre à X.," in *Le Collège de Sociologie (1937–1939)*, ed. Denis Hollier (Paris: Gallimard, 1995),

75–82, 76.

31. Georges Bataille, *L'expérience intérieure* (Paris: Gallimard, 1954), 49 (my translation).

32. Ibid., 85.

33. Ibid., 17.

34. I would like to thank the external reviewer for this Bataillean insight.

35. Bataille, *Erotism*, 11.

36. Bataille, Œuvres *complètes*, 7:245–46.

37. Nancy, *Inoperative Community*, 5.

38. Blanchot, *La communauté inavouable*, 23.

39. Miller, *The Conflagration of Community*, 16.

40. Nancy, *Inoperative Community*, 15.

41. Blanchot, *La communauté inavouable*, 22.

42. Bataille, Œuvres *complètes*, 1:348.

43. Ibid., 2:354.

44. Ibid., 1:470.

45. Georges Bataille, "What We Have Undertaken . . . ," in *The Obsessions of Georges Bataille*, ed. A. J. Mitchell and J. C. Winfree, trans. S. Kendall (Albany, NY: SUNY Press, 2009), 189–95, 192.

46. "Déclaration," in *Le Collège de Sociologie (1937–39)*, ed. Denis Hollier (Paris: Gallimard, 1995), 26–27, 26.

47. Hollier, *Le Collège*, 27, 8.

48. Denis Hollier, ed., *The College of Sociology, 1937–39*, trans. Betsy Wing (Minneapolis: Minnesota University Press, 1998).

49. See "Bataille and Heterology," ed. Roy Boyne and Marina Galletti, special issue, *Theory, Culture & Society* 35, no. 4–5 (2018).

50. See Michèle Richman, *Sacred Revolutions: Durkheim and the Collège de Sociologie* (Minneapolis: University of Minnesota Press, 2002).

51. Bataille, Œuvres *complètes*, 2:291.

52. Hollier, *College of Sociology*, 8.

53. Bataille, Œuvres *complètes*, 2:295.

54. Ibid.

55. Ibid.

56. Ibid., 2:338.

57. Girard, *Violence and the Sacred*, 8.

58. Bataille, Œuvres *complètes*, 2:325, 370.

59. Ibid., 2:300.

60. Ibid., 2:301.

61. Ibid., 2:302.

62. Blanchot, *La communauté inavouable*, 33.

63. Bataille, *Œuvres complètes*, 2:314.

64. Nancy, *Inoperative Community*, 32.

65. Philippe Lacoue-Labarthe and Jean-Luc Nancy, "The Nazi Myth," trans. B. Holmes, *Critical Inquiry* 16, no. 2 (1990): 291–312, 302.

66. Jacques Derrida, "From Restricted to General Economy: A Hegelianism without Reserve," in *Writing and Difference*, trans. A. Bass (Chicago: University of Chicago Press, 1978), 251–77.

67. Bataille, *Expérience intérieure*, 39, 23, 82.

68. See also Nidesh Lawtoo, "Bataille and the Homology of Heterology," *Theory, Culture and Society* 35, no. 4–5 (2018): 41–68.

69. Girard, *Evolution and Conversion*, 252.

70. Bataille, *Expérience intérieure* , 95, 64. This is arguably the unavowed source of Agamben's conception of "whatever being" (*essere qualunque*) that inaugurates *The Coming Community*, 1–3.

71. Bataille, *Expérience intérieure* , 74, 55.

72. Ibid., 39.

73. Ibid., 34.

74. Ibid., 112.

75. Ibid., 40.

76. Nancy, "The Common Growl," ix.

77. Judith Butler, *Notes toward a Performative Theory of Assembly* (Cambridge, MA: Harvard University Press, 2015); William E. Connolly, *Facing the Planetary: Entangled Humanism and the Politics of Swarming* (Durham, NC: Duke University Press, 2017).

78. Joining the notion of community to the one of crowd (*foule*), Girard adds: "The members of a crowd are always potential persecutors because they dream of purging [*purger*] the community of impure elements that corrupt it." René Girard, *Le bouc* émissaire (Paris: Grasset, 1982), 26.

79. Bataille, Œuvres *complètes*, 1:362.

80. Ibid., 1:357.

81. Blanchot, *La communauté inavouable*, 18.

82. Nancy, *Inoperative Community*, 20, 29.

83. Bataille, Œuvres *complètes*, 1:489, 453.

84. Ibid., 1:453.

85. Ibid., 2:302.

86. Girard, *Violence and the Sacred*, 222.

87. Nancy, *Inoperative Community*, 20.

88. Nancy recently acknowledges that in *The Inoperative Community* he "had neglected the Bataille of *Contre-attaque*" precisely because of the "misunderstanding that had appeared in reference to 'sur-fascism.'" Nancy, *The Disavowed Community*, 10.

89. Nancy, *Inoperative Community*, 20.

90. Girard, *Violence and the Sacred*, 37; translation modified.

91. Bataille, Œuvres *complètes*, 1:424–25.

92. Nancy, *Inoperative Community*, 20.

93. Ibid., 17.

94. Nancy, *The Disavowed Community*, 25; see also 12.

95. Girard, *Battling to the End*, 212.

96. Bataille, Œuvres *complètes*, 2:330.

97. Ibid., 1:367.

98. Ibid., 2:204.

99. Ibid., 2:224.

100. Connolly, *Aspirational Fascism*, 12–13.

101. Bataille, Œuvres *complètes*, 1:359.

102. Ibid., 1:403. See also Hal Foster, "Père Trump," *October* 159 (Winter 2017): 3–6, 5.

103. Bataille, Œuvres *complètes*, 1:348. For these lengthy quotes I rely on the following translation (and adapt it when necessary): Georges Bataille, "The Psychological Structure of Fascism," trans. Carl L. Lovitt, *New German Critique* 16 (Winter 1979): 64–87. For consistency page references are from the French original.

104. See also Georges Bataille, "The Notion of Expenditure," in *Critical Theory since Plato*, revised edition, ed. H. Adams, trans. A. Stoekl (Orlando: Harcourt Brace Jovanovich College Publishers, 1992), 857–64.

105. Bataille, Œuvres *complètes*, 2:344.

106. Ibid., 1:339.

107. Ibid., 1:348–49.

108. Ibid., 1:345.

109. Ibid., 1:353.

110. Bataille, "The Notion of Expenditure," 862.

111. Bataille, Œuvres *complètes*, 2:336.

112. Ibid., 1:246.

113. For a positive account of the role mimetic contagion plays in politics of swarming attentive to human and nonhuman processes, see Connolly, *Facing the Planetary*, chap. 5. Connolly and I will return to this in the coda.

114. Bataille, Œuvres *complètes*, 1:347, 353. See also Lawtoo, "Bataille and the Homology of Heterology."

115. Bataille, Œuvres *complètes*, 1:347.

116. Giacomo Rizzolatti and Corrado Sinigaglia, *Mirrors in the Brain: How Our Minds Share Actions and Emotions*, trans. F. Anderson (Oxford: Oxford University Press, 2008), 176–77.

117. Ibid., 191.

118. Girard, *Le bouc* émissaire, 26.

119. Bataille, Œuvres *complètes*, 1:359.

120. Bataille, *Erotism*, 164.

121. Bataille, Œuvres *complètes*, 2:302.

122. Nancy, "The Common Growl," ix.

123. Ibid.

Chapter 3. The Power of Myth Reloaded

1. Plato, *Ion*, trans. Lane Cooper, in *The Collected Dialogues of Plato*, ed. Edith Hamilton and Huntington Cairns (New York: Pantheon Books, 1961), 227.

2. Plato, *Republic*, trans. Paul Shorey, in *The Collected Dialogues of Plato*, ed. Edith Hamilton and Huntington Cairns (New York: Pantheon Books, 1961), 832.

3. Jean-Pierre Vernant, *Myth and Society in Ancient Greece*, trans. Janet Lloyd (Sussex: Harvester Press, 1980), 187.

4. With Plato, and later Aristotle, Vernant continues, "The *logos* is no longer simply speech but has come to imply demonstrative rationality and, as such, it is set in opposition, both in form and in fundamental significance, to the speech of *muthos*" (Vernant, *Myth and Society*, 188). See also Eric A. Havelock, *Preface to Plato* (Cambridge, MA: Harvard University Press, 1963), esp. chap. 2.

5. On Lacoue-Labarthe's take on poetics and politics, see *MLN* 132, no. 5 (2017).

6. See Girard, *"To Double Business Bound": Essays on Literature, Mimesis, and Anthropology* (Baltimore: Johns Hopkins University Press, 1988), 203–4; Philippe

Lacoue-Labarthe, "Typography," in *Typography: Mimesis, Philosophy, Politics*, ed. Christopher Fynsk (Cambridge, MA: Harvard University Press, 1989), 43–138, 110–15.

7. Girard, *To Double Business*, 203.

8. Philippe Lacoue-Labarthe and Jean-Luc Nancy, *Le mythe nazi* (La Tour d'Aigues: Éditions de l'Aube, 2016), 8. Unless specified otherwise, I will refer to the English translation, "The Nazi Myth," trans. Brian Holmes, *Critical Inquiry* 16, no. 2 (1990): 291–312.

9. Lacoue-Labarthe and Nancy, "The Nazi Myth," 294.

10. Jean-Luc Nancy, "Myth Interrupted," in *The Inoperative Community*, trans. Peter Connor (Minneapolis: University of Minnesota Press, 1991), 47, 46.

11. Friedrich Nietzsche, *Daybreak: Thoughts on the Prejudices of Morality*, trans. R. J. Hollingdale (Cambridge: Cambridge University Press, 1982), 106.

12. Philippe Lacoue-Labarthe, "Stagings of Mimesis, an Interview," trans. Jane Hiddleston, *Angelaki* 8, no. 2 (2003): 55–72, 65.

13. Ibid., 64, 65.

14. Ibid., 64.

15. Ibid., 64, 65.

16. Lacoue-Labarthe and Nancy, "The Nazi Myth," 312.

17. Lacoue-Labarthe and Nancy, *Le mythe nazi*, 16. The concept of "figura" for Lacoue-Labarthe cannot be dissociated from an identification with an authoritarian figure.

18. Donald J. Trump, *Great Again: How to Fix Our Crippled America* (New York: Threshold Editions, 2015), 3.

19. Noam Chomsky, *Requiem for the American Dream: The 10 Principles of Concentration of Wealth and Power* (New York: Seven Stories Press, 2017), x.

20. Hannah Arendt, *The Origins of Totalitarianism* (New York: A Harvest Book, 1976), 333.

21. George Mosse, *Nazi Culture: Intellectual, Cultural and Social Life in the Third Reich*, trans. Salvator Attanasio et al. (New York: Grosset & Dunlap, 1966), 96.

22. Ibid., xli.

23. Timothy Snyder, *On Tyranny: Twenty Lessons from the Twentieth Century* (New York: Tim Duggan Books, 2017), 12.

24. Ibid., 124.

25. William E. Connolly, *Aspirational Fascism: The Struggle for Multifaceted Democracy under Trumpism* (Minneapolis: University of Minnesota Press, 2018), 8.

26. Ibid., 8.

27. Lacoue-Labarthe and Nancy, "The Nazi Myth," 304.

28. Ibid.

29. Alfred Rosenberg, *The Myth of the 20th Century* (La Vergne, TN, 2016), 3, 12, 208.

30. Ibid., 5.

31. Ibid., 208.

32. Ibid., 13, 205.

33. Philippe Lacoue-Labarthe, *La fiction du politique: Heidegger, l'art et la politique* (Paris: Christian Bourgeois, 1987), 140. Unless specified otherwise, I will refer to the English translation, *Heidegger, Art and Politics: The Fiction of the Political*, trans. Chris Turner (New York: Blackwell, 1990), 97. On Rosenberg, see also 93–97.

34. Lacoue-Labarthe and Nancy, "The Nazi Myth," 294.

35. See Lacoue-Labarthe, "Typography," 43–138.

36. Lacoue-Labarthe and Nancy, "The Nazi Myth," 297.

37. The historian of religion Mircea Eliade calls this "the main

function of myth," namely, to "reveal the exemplary models of all rites and of all significant human activities"; if in his youth, Eliade flirted with fascist themes, he will later critique the "racist myth of 'Aryanism,' which is periodically revalued in the West, especially in Germany," as he writes: "The Aryan was the exemplary model to imitate in order to recuperate racial purity." Mircea Eliade, *Aspects du mythe* (Paris: Gallimard, 1963; my trans.), 19, 225.

38. Lacoue-Labarthe, *La fiction du politique*, 101.

39. Rosenberg, *The Myth of the 20th Century*, 10.

40. Ibid., 197; Jean-Luc Nancy and Philippe Lacoue-Labarthe, "The Jewish People Do Not Dream (Part One)," *Stanford Literary Review* 6, no. 2 (1989): 191–209.

41. Rosenberg, *The Myth of the 20th Century*, 198.

42. Lacoue-Labarthe and Nancy, "The Nazi Myth," 296, 306, 305.

43. Philippe Lacoue-Labarthe, "The Horror of the West," trans. Nidesh Lawtoo and Hannes Opelz; on Lacoue-Labarthe, fascism, and myth, see also Nidesh Lawtoo, "A Frame for 'The Horror of the West'"; both in Lawtoo, *Conrad's* Heart of Darkness *and Contemporary Thought: Revisiting*

the Horror with Lacoue-Labarthe (London: Bloomsbury, 2012), 111–22, 89–108.

44. Philippe Lacoue-Labarthe, *La réponse d'Ulysse: Et autres textes sur L'Occident*, ed. Aristide Bianchi and Leonid Kharlamov (Lignes/Imec, 2012), 90. This insight is arguably indebted to Girard's connection between the persecution of Jews and sacrifice in *Le bouc* émissaire (Paris: Grasset, 1982), chap. 1.

45. Connolly, *Aspirational Fascism*, 44.

46. Lacoue-Labarthe and Nancy, "The Nazi Myth," 305, 298.

47. Trump, *Great Again*, xii.

48. Nancy and Lacoue-Labarthe caution us against the danger of "democratic" countries who are "identified with a Commander in Chief [*chef d'Etat*], a flag, an army, an imagery," yet also specify that simple "returns or repetitions are rare, if not inexistent, in history." Lacoue-Labarthe and Nancy, *Le mythe nazi* 16, 13. On the similarities and differences between Trumpism and Nazism, see also Connolly, *Aspirational Fascism*, esp. 1–30.

49. Lacoue-Labarthe and Nancy, "The Nazi Myth," 312.

50. Sigmund Freud, *Group Psychology and the Analysis of the*

Ego, trans. James Strachey (New York: W.W. Norton, 1959), 38.

51. Mikkel Borch-Jacobsen, *The Freudian Subject*, trans. Catherine Porter (Stanford, CA: Stanford University Press, 1988), 10. See also Philippe Lacoue-Labarthe and Jean-Luc Nancy, "La panique politique," in *Retreating the Political*, ed. Simon Sparks (London: Routledge, 1977), 1–28.

52. Wilhelm Reich, *The Mass Psychology of Fascism*, trans. Theodore P. Wolfe (Delhi: Aakar Books, 2015), 74.

53. Lacoue-Labarthe and Nancy, "The Nazi Myth," 302.

54. Friedrich Nietzsche, *The Birth of Tragedy*, in *The Birth of Tragedy and The Case of Wagner*, trans. Walter Kaufmann (New York: Vintage Books, 1967), 34.

55. Rosenberg, *The Myth of the 20th Century*, 21, 22. As Bataille also noticed in his critique of Rosenberg's appropriation of Nietzsche, "fascism's hostility toward chthonic gods, the gods of the earth, is certainly what situates it in a psychological or mythological world." Georges Bataille, "Nietzsche et les fascistes," in *Œuvres complètes*, vol. 1 (Paris: Gallimard, 1970; my translation), 457; see also 455–58.

56. Rosenberg, *The Myth of the 20th Century*, 25.

57. Lacoue-Labarthe and Nancy, "The Nazi Myth," 301, 302.

58. Georges Bataille, "La structure psychologique du fascisme," in Œuvres *complètes*, 1:339–71.

59. On Trumpism and simulation, see Cynthia Weber, "The Trump Presidency, Episode 1: Simulating Sovereignty," *Theory & Event* 20, no. 1 (2017): 132–42. On hypermimesis as a form of simulation with real, all too real political effects, see Lawtoo, "Hypermimesis: Horrorism *Redux* in *The Secret Agent*," in *Conrad's Shadow: Catastrophe, Mimesis, Theory* (East Lansing: Michigan State University Press, 2016), 293–330.

60. Lacoue-Labarthe and Nancy, "The Nazi Myth," 298.

61. Lacoue-Labarthe, *La fiction du politique*, 77.

62. Friedrich Nietzsche, *The Gay Science*, trans. Walter Kaufmann (New York: Vintage Books, 1974), 316.

63. Nietzsche, *Gay Science*, 303.

64. Friedrich Nietzsche, *Twilight of the Idols*, in *The Portable Nietzsche*, ed. and trans. Walter Kaufmann (New York: Penguin Books, 1976), 463–563, 486.

65. Ibid., 486.

66. For a more detailed discussion of Nietzsche's anti-mimetic politics, see Nidesh Lawtoo, *The Phantom of the Ego: Modernism and the Mimetic Unconscious* (East Lansing: Michigan State University Press, 2013), 76–83.

67. Since I discussed comedy in the interview with William Connolly that follows, my position has shifted somewhat. While continuing to appreciate the anti-fascist unmasking operations of satirical shows at the level of the message, I have become more critical of comedians' complicity with the same hypermimetic medium responsible for turning tragic political actions into entertaining comedic reactions. I shall return to this elsewhere.

Coda. Fascism Now and Then: William Connolly and Nidesh Lawtoo in Conversation

The conversation between William Connolly and the author took place in Weimar in June 2017.

1. Since in *Aspirational Fascism* Bill Connolly capitalizes "Fascism," I have retained his rendering.

Bibliography

Adorno, Theodor W., Else Frenkel-Brunswik, Daniel J. Levinson, and R. Nevitt Sanford. *The Authoritarian Personality*. New York: Harper and Brothers, 1950.

Agamben, Giorgio. *The Coming Community*. Translated by Michael Hardt. Minneapolis: University of Minnesota Press, 1993.

Anderson, Benedict. *Imagined Communities: Reflections on the Origins and Spread of Nationalism*. London: Verso, 1983.

Arendt, Hannah. *The Origins of Totalitarianism*. New York: A Harvest Book, 1976.

Barthes, Roland. "From Work to Text." In *Image, Music, Text*. Edited and translated by Stephen Heath, 155–64. London: Fontana Press, 1977.

Bataille, George. *Erotism: Death and Sensuality*. Translated by

Mary Dalwood. San Francisco: City Lights Books, 1986.

———. *L'expérience intérieure*. Paris: Gallimard, 1954.

———. "Lettre à X." In *Le Collège de Sociologie (1937–1939)*. Edited by Denis Hollier, 75–82. Paris: Gallimard, 1995.

———. "The Notion of Expenditure." In *Critical Theory since Plato*. Rev. ed. Edited by H. Adams. Translated by Allan Stoekl, 857–64. Orlando, FL: Harcourt Brace Jovanovich College Publishers, 1992.

———. Œuvres *complètes*. 12 vols. Paris: Gallimard, 1970–88.

———. "The Psychological Structure of Fascism." Translated by Carl L. Lovitt. *New German Critique* 16 (Winter 1979): 64–87.

———. "What We Have Undertaken. . . ." In *The Obsessions of Georges Bataille*, translated by Stuart Kendall, edited by Andrew J. Mitchell and Jason Camp Winfree, 189–95. Albany, NY: SUNY Press, 2009.

Baudrillard, Jean. *In the Shadow of the Silent Majorities*. Translated by Paul Foss et al. Los Angeles: Semiotext(e), 2007.

Bernays, Edward. *Propaganda*. New York: Ig Publishing, 2005.

Blanchot, Maurice. *La communauté inavouable*. Paris: Les

Éditions de Minuit, 1983.

Borch, Christian, ed. *Imitation, Contagion, Suggestion: On Mimesis and Society*. New York: Routledge, 2019.

Borch, Christian. *The Politics of Crowds: An Alternative History of Sociology*. Cambridge: Cambridge University Press, 2012.

Borch-Jacobsen, Mikkel. *The Emotional Tie: Psychoanalysis, Mimesis, and Affect*. Translated by Douglas Brick. Stanford, CA: Stanford University Press, 1992.

——. *The Freudian Subject*. Translated by Catherine Porter. Stanford, CA: Stanford University Press, 1988.

Boyne, Roy, and Marina Galletti, eds. "Bataille and Heterology." Special issue, *Theory, Culture & Society* 35, no. 4–5 (2018).

Butler, Judith. *Notes toward a Performative Theory of Assembly*. Cambridge, MA: Harvard University Press, 2015.

Cadava, Eduardo, Peter Connor, and Jean-Luc Nancy, eds. *Who Comes after the Subject?* New York: Routledge, 1991.

Canetti, Elias. *Crowds and Power*. Translated by Carol Stewart. New York: Ferrar, Straus and Giroux, 1962.

Chomsky, Noam. *Requiem for the American Dream: The 10 Principles of Concentration of Wealth and Power*. New York: Seven Stories Press, 2017.

Connolly, William E. *Aspirational Fascism: The Struggle for Multifaceted Democracy under Trumpism.* Minneapolis: University of Minnesota Press, 2018.

———. *Facing the Planetary: Entangled Humanism and the Politics of Swarming.* Durham, NC: Duke University Press, 2017.

Derrida, Jacques. "From Restricted to General Economy: A Hegelianism without Reserve." In *Writing and Difference,* edited and translated by Alan Bass. Chicago: University of Chicago Press, 1978.

Dumouchel, Paul. "Massengewalt und konstitutive Gewalt." In *Gewaltmassen: Ueber Eigendynamik und Selbstorganisation kollektiver Gewalt*, edited by Axel T. Paul and Benjamin Schwalb, 103–23. Hamburg: Hamburger Edition, 2015.

Dupuy, Jean-Pierre. *Dans l'oeil du cyclone: Colloque de Cerisy.* Paris: Carnet Nord, 2008.

———. *La panique.* Paris: Seuil, 2003.

Eco, Umberto. "Ur-Fascism." *New York Review of Books*, June 22, 1995.

Eliade, Mircea. *Aspects du mythe.* Paris: Gallimard, 1963.

Ffrench, Patrick. *After Bataille: Sacrifice, Exposure, Community.*

London: Legenda, 2007.

Foster, Hal. "Père Trump." *October* 159 (Winter 2017): 3–6.

Freud, Sigmund. *Group Psychology and the Analysis of the Ego*. Translated by James Strachey. New York: W.W. Norton & Co., 1959.

———. *Totem and Taboo*. Translated by A. A. Brill. Harmondsworth, UK: Penguin, 1940.

Gallese, Vittorio. "The Two Sides of Mimesis: Mimetic Theory, Embodied Simulation, and Social Identification." In *Mimesis and Science: Empirical Research on Imitation and the Mimetic Theory of Culture and Religion*, edited by Scott Garrels, 87–108. East Lansing: Michigan State University Press, 2011.

Girard, René. *Battling to the End*. Translated by Mary Baker. East Lansing: Michigan State University Press, 2010.

———. *Le bouc émissaire*. Paris: Grasset, 1982.

———. *Deceit, Desire and the Novel: Self and Other in Literary Structure*. Translated by Yvonne Freccero. Baltimore: Johns Hopkins University Press, 1965.

———. *Des choses cachées depuis la fondation du monde*. Paris: Editions Grasset, 1978.

———. *Evolution and Conversion: Dialogues on the Origins of Culture*. With Pierpaolo Antonello and João de Castro Rocha. London: Continuum, 2007.

———. *"To Double Business Bound": Essays on Literature, Mimesis, and Anthropology*. Baltimore: Johns Hopkins University Press, 1988.

———. *Violence and the Sacred*. Translated by Patrick Gregory. Baltimore: Johns Hopkins University Press, 1977.

Griffin, Roger, ed. *International Fascism: Theory, Causes and the New Consensus*. London: Arnold, 1998.

Griffin, Roger, and Matthew Feldman, eds. *Fascism: Critical Concepts in Political Science*. Vol. 3. London: Routledge, 2004.

Havelock, Eric A. *Preface to Plato*. Cambridge, MA: Harvard University Press, 1963.

Hollier, Denis, ed. *Le Collège de Sociologie, 1937–39*. Paris: Gallimard, 1995.

———, ed. *The College of Sociology, 1937–39*. Translated by Betsy Wing. Minneapolis: Minnesota University Press, 1998.

Lacoue-Labarthe, Philippe. *La fiction du politique: Heidegger, l'art et la politique*. Paris: Christian Bourgeois, 1987.

———. *Heidegger, Art and Politics: The Fiction of the Political.*
Translated by Chris Turner. New York: Blackwell, 1990.

———. "The Horror of the West." Translated by Nidesh Lawtoo
and Hannes Opelz. In *Conrad's* Heart of Darkness *and
Contemporary Thought: Revisiting the Horror with Lacoue-
Labarthe*, edited by Nidesh Lawtoo, 111–22. London:
Bloomsbury, 2012.

———. *L'imitation des modernes (Typographies II)*. Paris:
Galilée, 1986.

———. *La réponse d'Ulysse: Et autres textes sur L'Occident.*
Edited by Aristide Bianchi and Leonid Kharlamov.
Fécamp, France: Lignes/Imec, 2012.

———. "Stagings of Mimesis, an Interview." Translated by Jane
Hiddleston. *Angelaki* 8, no. 2 (2003): 55–72.

———. *Typography: Mimesis, Philosophy, Politics.* Edited by
Christopher Fynsk. Cambridge, MA: Harvard University
Press, 1989.

Lacoue-Labarthe, Philippe, and Jean-Luc Nancy. *Le mythe nazi.*
La Tour d'Aigues, France: Éditions de l'Aube, 2016.

———. "The Nazi Myth." Translated by Brian Holmes. *Critical*

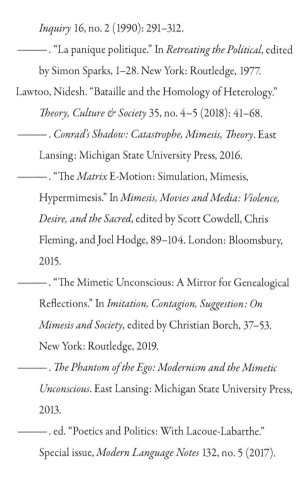
Inquiry 16, no. 2 (1990): 291–312.

———. "La panique politique." In *Retreating the Political*, edited by Simon Sparks, 1–28. New York: Routledge, 1977.

Lawtoo, Nidesh. "Bataille and the Homology of Heterology." *Theory, Culture & Society* 35, no. 4–5 (2018): 41–68.

———. *Conrad's Shadow: Catastrophe, Mimesis, Theory*. East Lansing: Michigan State University Press, 2016.

———. "The *Matrix* E-Motion: Simulation, Mimesis, Hypermimesis." In *Mimesis, Movies and Media: Violence, Desire, and the Sacred*, edited by Scott Cowdell, Chris Fleming, and Joel Hodge, 89–104. London: Bloomsbury, 2015.

———. "The Mimetic Unconscious: A Mirror for Genealogical Reflections." In *Imitation, Contagion, Suggestion: On Mimesis and Society*, edited by Christian Borch, 37–53. New York: Routledge, 2019.

———. *The Phantom of the Ego: Modernism and the Mimetic Unconscious*. East Lansing: Michigan State University Press, 2013.

———. ed. "Poetics and Politics: With Lacoue-Labarthe." Special issue, *Modern Language Notes* 132, no. 5 (2017).

———. "Violence and the Mimetic Unconscious, Part One: The Cathartic Hypothesis (Aristotle, Freud, Girard)." *Contagion* 25 (2018): 159–92.

———. "Violence and the Mimetic Unconscious Part Two: The Contagious Hypothesis (Plato, Affect, Mirror Neurons)." *Contagion* 26 (2019).

Le Bon, Gustave. *Psychologie des foules*. Paris: Presses Universitaires de France, 1963.

Miller, Hillis J. *The Conflagration of Community: Fiction before and after Auschwitz*. Chicago: University of Chicago Press, 2011.

Mitchell, Andres J., and Jason Kemp Winfree, eds. *The Obsessions of Georges Bataille: Community and Communication*. Albany, NY: SUNY Press, 2009.

Moscovici, Serge. *The Age of the Crowd: A Historical Treatise on Mass Psychology*. Translated by J. C. Whitehouse. Cambridge: Cambridge University Press, 1985.

Mosse, George. *The Fascist Revolution: Toward a General Theory of Fascism*. New York: Howard Fertig, 1999.

———. *Nazi Culture: Intellectual, Cultural, and Social Life in the Third Reich*. Translated by Salvator Attanasio et al. New

York: Grosset & Dunlap, 1966.

Mussolini, Benito, and Giovanni Gentile. *La dottrina del fascismo* (1932). http://www.polyarchy.org/basta/documenti/fascismo.1932.html.

Nancy, Jean-Luc. *Being Singular Plural*. Translated by Robert D. Richardson and Anne E. O'Byrne. Stanford, CA: Stanford University Press, 2000.

——. "The Common Growl." In *The Common Growl: Toward a Poetics of Precarious Community*, edited by Thomas Claviez and translated by Steven Corcoran, vii–ix. New York: Fordham University Press, 2016.

——. *The Disavowed Community*. Translated by Paul Armstrong. New York: Fordham University Press, 2016.

——. *The Inoperative Community*. Edited by Peter Connor. Translated by Peter Connor et al. Minneapolis: University of Minnesota Press, 1991.

Nancy, Jean-Luc, and Philippe Lacoue-Labarthe. "The Jewish People Do Not Dream (Part One)." *Stanford Literary Review* 6, no. 2 (1989): 191–209.

Nietzsche, Friedrich. *The Birth of Tragedy*. In *The Birth of Tragedy and The Case of Wagner*, translated by Walter

Kaufmann. New York: Vintage Books, 1967.

———. *Daybreak: Thoughts on the Prejudices of Morality.* Translated by R. J. Hollingdale. Cambridge: Cambridge University Press, 1982.

———. *The Gay Science.* Translated by Walter Kaufmann. New York: Vintage Books, 1974.

———. *On the Genealogy of Morals.* Translated by Douglas Smith. Oxford: Oxford University Press, 1998.

———. *Twilight of the Idols.* In *The Portable Nietzsche*, edited and translated by Walter Kaufmann, 463–563. New York: Penguin Books, 1976.

Passmore, Kevin. *Fascism: A Very Short Introduction.* Oxford: Oxford University Press, 2002.

Paxton, Robert O. *The Anatomy of Fascism.* New York: Alfred A. Knopf, 2004.

Plato. *The Collected Dialogues of Plato.* Edited by Edith Hamilton and Huntington Cairns. New York: Pantheon Books, 1961.

Reich, Wilhelm. *The Mass Psychology of Fascism.* Translated by Theodore P. Wolfe. Delhi: Aakar Books, 2015.

Richman, Michèle. *Sacred Revolutions: Durkheim and the Collège de Sociologie.* Minneapolis: University of Minnesota Press, 2002.

Rizzolatti, Giacomo, and Corrado Sinigaglia. *Mirrors in the Brain: How Our Minds Share Actions and Emotions.* Translated by Frances Anderson. Oxford: Oxford University Press, 2008.

Rosenberg, Alfred. *The Myth of the 20th Century.* La Vergne, TN, 2016.

Sloterdijk, Peter. *Die Verachtung der Massen: Versuch über Kulturkämpfe in der modernen Gesellschaft.* Frankfurt: Suhrkamp, 2000.

Snyder, Timothy. *Black Earth: The Holocaust as History and Warning.* London: Bodley Head, 2015.

——. *The Road to Unfreedom: Russia, Europe, America.* London: Penguin, 2018.

——. *On Tyranny: Twenty Lessons from the Twentieth Century.* New York: Tim Duggan Books, 2017.

Tarde, Gabriel. *Les lois de l'imitation.* Paris: Seuil, 2001.

——. *L'opinion et la foule.* Paris: Félix Alcan Editeur, 1901.

Tönnies, Ferdinand. *Community and Society.* Edited and translated by Charles P. Loomis. New York: Dover

Publications, 1963.

Traylor, Anthony D. "Violence Has Its Reasons: Girard and Bataille." *Contagion* 21 (2014): 131–56.

Trump, Donald J. *Great Again: How to Fix Our Crippled America*. New York: Threshold Editions, 2015.

Vernant, Jean-Pierre. *Myth and Society in Ancient Greece*. Translated by Janet Lloyd. Sussex, UK: Harvester Press, 1980.

Weber, Cynthia. "The Trump Presidency, Episode 1: Simulating Sovereignty." *Theory & Event* 20, no. 1 (2017): 132–42.